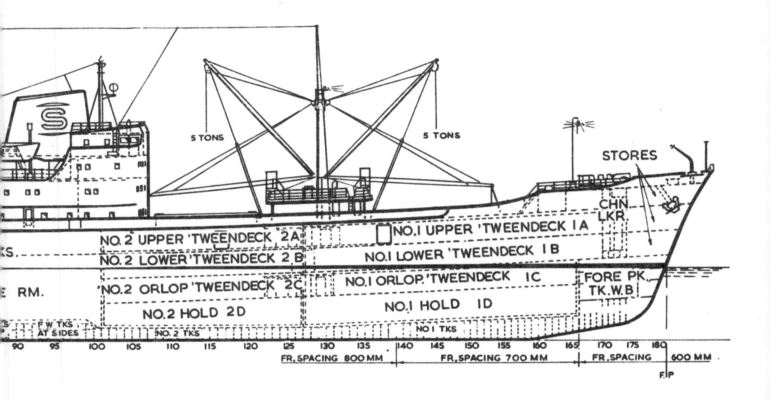

5 TONS   5 TONS

STORES

CHN
LKR

S

NO. 2 UPPER 'TWEENDECK 2A   NO.1 UPPER 'TWEENDECK 1A
KS.   NO. 2 LOWER 'TWEENDECK 2 B   NO.1 LOWER 'TWEENDECK 1 B

RM.   NO.2 ORLOP 'TWEENDECK 2C   NO.1 ORLOP 'TWEENDECK 1C   FORE PK.
                                                                        TK. W.B
          NO. 2 HOLD 2D   NO.1 HOLD 1D

S   F W TKS   NO I TKS
         AT SIDES   NO. 2 TKS

90   95   100   105   110   115   120   125   130   135   140 145   150   155   160   165   170   175   180

FR. SPACING 800 MM   FR. SPACING 700 MM   FR. SPACING   600 MM

F.P

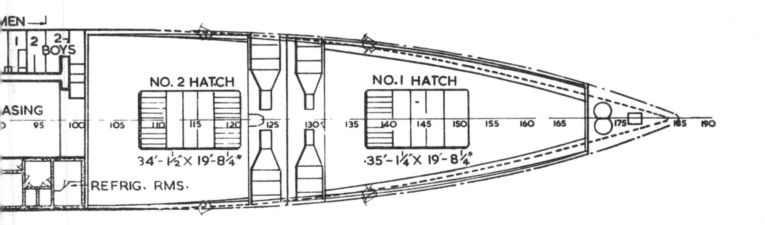

MEN

1   2   2
       BOYS   NO. 2 HATCH   NO.1 HATCH

ASING   STORES
                                                                                                    175

95   100   105   110   115   120   125   130   135   140   145   150   155   160   165   175   185   190

                    34'-1½" X 19'-8¼"   ·35'-1¼" X 19'-8¼"

         REFRIG. RMS.

REEFER SHIPS

THE OCEAN PRINCESSES

NICK TOLERTON

CONTENTS

Introduction 7

Refrigerated Ship Evolution and Development 9

The Classic European Reefers 17

Modern Western European-Built Reefers 47

Soviet and East European Reefers 59

Japanese-Built Reefers 69

The Drammen Reefers 83

Maritime Fruit Carriers and the Core Ships 99

J Lauritzen 109

Salenrederierna 129

Cool Carriers 139

The Erikson Reefers 141

The P&O Group's Reefers 145

Blue Star and Star Reefers 155

Geest Line 169

Seatrade Groningen 177

The Great White Fleets -- United Fruit, Chiquita, and Fyffes 185

Laskaridis Shipping 199

Reefers in Colour 200

Bibliography & Acknowledgements 215

Index of Ship Names 217

Speed, bonny boat -- AP Moller's *Dragor Maersk* of 1961, typical of the classic reefers of a generation past, gathers pace outward bound from a New Zealand port. (Tolerton)

INTRODUCTION

Everyone with an interest in ships and the sea has his own favourite vessels, be they merchant or naval. In this author's case it is reefers, and that traces back to a particular ship -- watching the *Dragor Maersk* accelerating down Lyttelton harbour with élan on a sunny late autumn day in 1971.

Pure reefers and fruitships were in those days not frequent visitors to New Zealand ports. Her sky blue Moller hull in less than pristine condition, she was nevertheless a picture of purpose, gathering speed more like a sports car than a conventional cargo ship, and a contrast to the stately progress in and out of port of the big refrigerated cargo liners of New Zealand Shipping, Shaw Savill, and the other companies that dominated the overseas trade in those days. Not surprisingly, there is a tangible esprit de corps among seafarers who crewed on reefers and fruitships -- a certainty that their vessels were the princesses of the seas.

This book is <u>not</u> a technical history of marine refrigeration. Rather it is a celebration of a century and a quarter of refrigerated shipping history, and a look at the vessels and the companies that have made this realm of shipping such a fascinating area for anyone with an interest in *res nautica*.

Refrigerated shipping attracted some of shipping's most dynamic entrepreneurs, the likes of Sven Salen, Sir Alfred Jones, Ivar and Knud Lauritzen, and in the past led to the construction of some of the world's most beautiful ships.

In the first decade of the 21st century it has seen enormous change, with a kaleidoscope of takeovers and mergers transforming this sector of maritime transport.

Refrigerated trade by sea has grown steadily over the last 12 years or so, but there has been next to no investment in new conventional reefer tonnage this decade as container ships take a larger and larger share of the market.

Some see in ships an expression of the hand of God working through man. Certainly, like the clipper ship of an earlier era, the traditional reefer ship with its white hull and graceful lines has been a creation to warm the hearts of both seafarers and pierhead observers of the passing maritime parade

Port Morant (1901/2830gt)

A historic day -- the Imperial Direct West India Line's little *Port Morant* locks out at Avonmouth on February 16, 1901, on her way to Jamaica to load the first Caribbean banana cargo for Britain. (Bristol Museums Galleries & Archives)

CHAPTER ONE

REFRIGERATED SHIP EVOLUTION AND DEVELOPMENT

The development of refrigerated shipping has not been indispensable to world commerce in the way that the advent of the box and the development of bulk oil and dry bulk transport by sea have been. However, thanks to it once-unheard of commodities like bananas, pineapples, oranges, and more recently exotics like kiwifruit have in the last 100 years become basic foodstuffs of consumer societies around the globe. The successful development of refrigerated transport by sea also laid the foundation of the prosperity of a number of countries ranging from New Zealand to Central American and Caribbean nations.

Finding a way to link the primary producers of Australia, New Zealand, and Argentina to the enormous consumer markets of Britain and Europe gave the development of marine refrigeration its impetus. The pasturelands of the young southern hemisphere countries sustained huge numbers of cattle and sheep. At the other end of the world was a market for it in the Victorian industrial cities. How to get mutton and beef to them other than in the less than satisfactory form of a canned product was the challenge for scientists and engineers. The world's first freezing works was established at Sydney in 1861, and experiments to ship frozen meat to Britain were made in the next decade.

In 1873 an Australian pioneer James Harrison attempted the shipment from Melbourne to London of a small cargo of mutton and beef frozen in two tanks on the auxiliary steamer *Norfolk*, but the meat went bad. Also unsuccessful was a project by Thomas Mort -- the builder of that first freezing works -- for the former P&O steamer *Northam* to carry a cargo of frozen meat from Sydney in 1876. Problems with the equipment meant the ship had to sail without the meat.

The French experimented more successfully. Engineer Charles Tellier acquired the 653gt Elder Dempster West African feeder steamer *Eboe* which was renamed *Frigorifique* and fitted with methyl ether machinery and cork insulation. She sailed from Rouen in 1876 to Buenos Aires with a small cargo of refrigerated meat, the voyage taking more than 100 days, and returned the following year with a cargo of 25 tons of chilled beef in good condition. More emphatic success came in 1878 when the Chargeurs Reunis steamer *Paraguay*, fitted with Ferdinand Carre ammonia machinery, carried 150 tons of frozen beef from Marseilles to Buenos Aires, returning to Le Havre with 80 tons of mutton. The meat was delivered in fine condition after both voyages, and marine refrigeration was successfully established.

More milestone voyages followed quickly. The Barrow Steam Ship Co's *Circassia* of 1878 with Bell Coleman machinery and space for 400 carcasses introduced refrigeration to the North Atlantic run for the Anchor Line, and in November the next year an even larger passenger steamer,

Orient Line's 5386gt *Orient* (then second only to the *Great Eastern* in size) and also fitted with Bell Coleman refrigeration, started her maiden voyage to Australia. But before that Australian pastoralists, aware of the huge possibilities for their country, had taken note of the successful voyage of the *Paraguay* and chartered the steamer *Strathleven*, in which Bell Coleman equipment had been installed, to carry 50 tons of frozen beef and mutton. She left Sydney in November 1879 and arrived in London in February 1880 with the meat in excellent condition. A more ambitious voyage with the *Protos* carrying 4600 mutton and lamb carcasses and 100 tons of butter followed, reaching London early in 1881.

Marine refrigeration was to transform another country's economy even more dramatically. The Albion Line's full-rigged ship *Dunedin* was fitted with Bell Coleman machinery to carry the first frozen meat cargo from the colony of New Zealand, sailing from Port Chalmers to London, where the cargo of 4909 carcasses of mutton and lamb and 22 pigs was received in perfect condition in May 1882. More vessels were quickly converted for the trade. The German *Marsala* was the first steamer in 1882, but her refrigeration machinery failed on the voyage. New Zealand Shipping Co's pioneer was the barque *Mataura*, fitted with Haslam dry air equipment, which arrived in London from Port Chalmers just a few months after the *Dunedin*. NZSCo's first steamer, the *Tongariro*, was delivered the following year with about 2430cu/m of freezer space. New Zealand was on its way to becoming the world's premier meat exporting country.

Today it is easy to forget how momentous these developments were for Australia and particularly for New Zealand -- and for their mother country 12,000 miles away by sea. A colony struggling to pay its way with wool its only other foreign exchange earner almost overnight had an economic raison d'être. And for Victorian Britain, meat was no longer just an expensive luxury.

Coinciding as it did with the improvements to compound machinery for steam ships, the refrigerated trades to South America, Australia, and New Zealand developed very rapidly. However, the great refrigerated liners on these routes in the decades to follow were invariably hybrids, with extensive uninsulated capacity for general cargoes as well as their deep refrigerated holds for meat, butter, and cheese. A major class of refrigerated liner, NZSCo's postwar 11,200gt H class like the *Haparangi* of 1947, had a two-thirds/one-third split of insulated and uninsulated capacity. The refrigerated cargo liner acme probably came with the Port Line's 21kn, 18,030gt *Port Chalmers* and *Port Caroline* of 1968, with their 18,779 cu/m of insulated space. However, with the box boat era starting they were almost obsolete when they went into service.

While the answers had been found to shipping frozen foodstuffs and steadily larger refrigerated ships were built particularly for the run to Australia and New Zealand, there was another challenge waiting for shipowners and marine refrigeration engineers as the end of the Victorian era approached.

That was the carriage of bananas under insulation, and was tackled separately on opposite sides of the Atlantic by American giant United Fruit and British shipping entrepreneur Sir Alfred Jones -- two empires that were to be joined a few years after Sir Alfred's death in 1909. In the first years of the 20th century both started successfully shipping this novel fruit from Caribbean plantations under refrigeration -- and, as with the shipment of frozen meat, helped transform the diets of ordinary people in the USA, Britain, and Europe.

The pioneering voyage in this field came in 1901 with the arrival at Bristol of the new refrigerated ship *Port Morant* of Sir Alfred Jones' Imperial Direct West India Line, carrying 18,000 stems of bananas. The successors of the *Port Morant*, particularly the fast fruit carriers of the 1950s and 60s, were to be some of the most attractive merchant ships ever built.

Classic banana boats -- Elders & Fyffes' *Bayano* (1917/6815gt) and *Carare* (1925/6878gt) coaling at Avonmouth. The latter was a war loss in 1940, mined close to home in the Bristol Channel, while the *Bayano* lasted until 1956 as the veteran of the fleet. (Bristol Museums Galleries & Archives)

Matangi -- The Cunard Steam-Ship Co, UK; Harland & Wolff, Belfast, 1961; 8297/10,486gt, 12,417dwt; 152m, 6ha (5ho), 1x75 4x15 5x10 7x5 & 2x3tn der, 11,500hp H&W-B&W, 17kn. (Tolerton)

One of the last of the traditional refrigerated cargo liners -- the *Matangi* was Port Line's *Port St Lawrence* of 1961, changing name in 1975 and adopting a Brocklebank Line funnel within the Cunard group. She had 12,502 cu/m of reefer space -- about two thirds of her cargo capacity -- and was probably the last traditional British cargo liner to visit New Zealand ports under the Red Duster, making her last call in 1982 just before being sold as the *Nordave* to Maltese owners. Early the next year she went to Gadani Beach.

P&O Nedlloyd Remuera -- **KG ms 'Santa Rafaela' Offen Reederei GmbH (Claus-Peter Offen), Liberia; Samsung HI, Koje, 2002; 45,803gt, 53,328dwt, 281m, 69,930hp Samsung-Sulzer, 25kn. (PONL)**

P&O Nedlloyd promoted the *P&O Nedlloyd Remuera* class as the world's biggest refrigerated container ships when a series of 10 ships (seven for PONL) was introduced with this vessel, launched as the *Santa Rafaela* and chartered from German owner Claus-Peter Offen, in 2002. The ship could carry 1300 reefer containers on deck in a complement of 4112 TEUs. Her impressive 25kn speed capability had an inevitable kicker -- fuel consumption of up to 185tn a day.

Bananas became the most important cargo for pure reefer ships, but had to be carried at a constant and exact temperature if excessive ripening aboard the ship was to be avoided. From the first relatively primitive shipments evolved special vessels with more and more fined technology for carrying this fruit at the critical temperature of about 12deg C. Every year more than 12 million tonnes of bananas are moved worldwide. Among the most sensitive of refrigerated cargoes, they are also the only significant fruit cargo to be shipped 12 months of the year -- providing assured business whatever the seasonal vagaries of other commodities. Their carriage made the fortunes of a number of shipowners.

The two threads in the marine refrigeration story were to eventually join with the advent of advanced reefers in the 1960s and 1970s able to carry cargoes through a wide range of temperatures and suitable for both fruit and meat.

After the arrival of the first banana boats, there were no enormous changes in the refrigerated trades until after World War Two, apart from the development of chilled meat carriage -- chilled meat being more appealing to the UK consumer than frozen meat. But after World War Two the growth of consumer societies saw the world fleet of pure reefers also grow steadily. The ships become larger and faster with more sophisticated cargo systems, too.

In the 1960s reefers capable of carrying cargo at different temperatures appeared, giving owners much more flexibility. Pure reefers could now carry a variety of cargoes. J Lauritzen's *Italian Reefer* of 1968, for example, the first of a class of six ships, had 15 cargo compartments each with its own refrigeration unit. Individual temperatures ranging from plus 16deg C to minus 25deg could be maintained in eight separate gas-tight sections

Ships being completed from the mid-1980s were invariably designed specifically for pallet carriage, with hold compartments having a clear deck height of 2.2m to maximise stowage. In the late 80s-early 90s reefers like the Salen Snow class and Blue Star's A class (all vessels built 1972-76) and big Japanese reefers like the *Royal Lily* (now *Cap Ortegal*) of 1979 were having to be modified to remain competitive on the major fruit trades.

More recently the introduction of controlled atmosphere provided another innovation in refrigeration technology, enabling even finer tuning of the carriage of the most sensitive perishables like grapes, lettuce, avocados, asparagus, and some fruits.

While the pure reefer ship has grown more and more sophisticated, looming over every development has been competition from the container ship. As well as on the reefer trades from more advanced countries like South Africa, Australia, and New Zealand, containers are now the norm for fruit shipments from the Caribbean and Central American countries. Today more than three-quarters of the world's reefer shipping capacity is container, and there is a question mark against the future of the conventional reefer. Significantly, the world's largest container shipping operator, Maersk, in 2001 had more than double the reefer capacity of either LauritzenCool or Seatrade, the two leading specialist reefer operators.

The containerisation of refrigerated cargoes saw two basic types of container evolve, one with its own integral refrigerating machinery, and the other an insulated box with ventilating ports to plug in to a shipboard ducting system.

Swift containerisation of the Australian and New Zealand export meat trades saw off the conventional refrigerated cargo liner after almost 100 years in which the funnels of great companies like Shaw Savill, NZSCo, Blue Star, and Port Line dominated the ports Down Under, and other traditional trades disappeared one by one for the reefer.

The first ACT container ships carried 326 reefer TEUs, while their *Encounter Bay* class contemporaries of OCL could carry 304. These early ships were soon outclassed by vessels like the *Remuera Bay* (1973) with 1151, the *Table Bay* (1977) and *City of Durban* (1978) with 941, the *Resolution Bay* (1977) with 1220, and the *Mairangi Bay* (1978) with 1273.

Meanwhile CGM explored the potential of containerisation for the West Indies banana trade with the *Fort Royal* of 1979, which could carry 754 ducted reefer containers below deck and another 51 self-contained reefer boxes on the hatch covers.

Before P&O Nedlloyd's disappearance from container shipping, the company lauded its new 25kn, 45,000gt *P&O Nedlloyd Remuera* class container ships from Samsung introduced from 2002 as the world's largest refrigerated container ships. Intended for a round-the-world service, they could each carry 1300 reefer containers in a complement of 4100 TEUs. The containers all had their own power plugs, whereas their predecessors in the New Zealand-Europe trade were "blown air." PONL invested US $200 million alone on the 14,500 integral 20 and 40ft reefer containers for these ships, only to dispose of its container fleet to Maersk in 2005.

PONL's "biggest" claim for them could be contested by Dole Fresh Fruit International on the strength of its innovative 1999 completions *Dole Chile* and *Dole Colombia* from Howaldtswerke-Deutsche Werft, Kiel. Although considerably smaller in their dimensions and tonnages than the PONL ships, these 31,799gt ships were indisputably the largest pure reefer container ships, designed for 1023 FEUs (equivalent to 2046 TEUs) and with approximately 60,000 cu/m refrigerated capacity. The six holds were served by two 40tn Liebherr gantry cranes. The size of these ships was not the only remarkable thing about them. Dole, which is now significantly ahead of the traditional kingpin

Chiquita as the leading supplier to the US banana market, opted for a hatchcoverless design apart from pontoon hatch covers for No.1 hold. HDW had pioneered the coverless concept on previous container ships, but not vessels this large. And with a full complement of reefer containers in the holds of such a large ship, special attention had to be given to ventilation, and Dole and HDW opted for integrated units with a new water cooling system.

Pure reefer shipping has never been the easiest segment of the maritime industry for an owner to operate in, and has been dominated by a very small number for most of its history. Reefer ships represent only a very small portion of the world merchant fleet -- about 1200 in service in 2003 -- but are expensive and sophisticated vessels. Owners have been determined to sustain them in service as long as possible. Historically the trade has been very vulnerable to overtonnaging -- the early 1980s were a time of over-capacity after many new and larger ships came into service, and the end of last century and early years of the new also saw depressed rates and lay-ups.

Over the years, major owners like J Lauritzen have typically looked to spread their risks with a fairly even split of owned and chartered vessels in their fleets. The difficulties were underlined anew in 2007 by the announcements by perhaps the two most famous reefer companies on either side of the Atlantic that they were withdrawing from owning. First the Great White Fleet sold its 12 ships, opting to lease vessels instead. Then, with even more seismic impact, Lauritzen announced it was quitting reefer shipping altogether to concentrate on its presumably more lucrative and reliable dry bulk and tanker interests.

Orders for conventional reefer ships have virtually dried up this decade. The delivery of four new ships to Star Reefers from Shikoku in 2006 (with a contract signed a year later for another quartet from the same yard) provided the only newbuildings of note.

While more and more of the traditional reefer trades have been containerised, there has still been a role for the conventional ship to work ports or trades less suitable for boxes (although these have been greatly reduced), and to serve on other routes at times of peak seasonal demand. Steady annual reefer trade growth helped by the increasing prosperity of the populations of East Asia and Russia has been the saving of some conventional reefers. However, the reduced role for the conventional ship and the dearth of new construction suggest that the traditional reefer, for so long among the most attractive sights on the world's seaways, may eventually be relegated to a place in nautical history like that of the clipper ships.

Reifu -- **Ubin Shipping Pte (Korea Marine), Singapore; Shin Kurushima, Hashihama, 1996; 3767gt, 4241dwt, 10m, 4ha, 8x5tn der, 4200hp Makita-B&W, 15kn. (Tolerton)**

Japanese-built ships like the fish carrier *Reifu*, built as the *Baystars II*, make up a large part of the world reefer fleet today. With an array of derricks that would gladden the heart of any old seafarer, she's relatively slow at 15kn but burns a miserly 12tn of fuel a day.

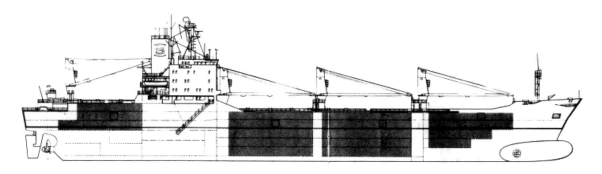

Winter class, **11,700gt (*The Motor Ship*)**

Conventional pure reefer ship design reached its peak with ships like Salen's six 22kn Winter class ships from Gotaverken in 1979-1980.

15

Elsfleth -- **Vosporos Shipping SA (Enterprises Shipping & Trading), Greece; Ch Nav de Flandre, Bruges, 1962; 4390gt, 4900dwt, 139m, 4ha, 8x5tn der, 7200bhp Borsig, 18kn. (Tolerton)**

Reefer perfection -- Bremen owner Scipio & Co's *Elsfleth* of 1962 under later Greek ownership, but retaining her original name. She went to Gadani Beach in 1984.

CHAPTER TWO

THE CLASSIC EUROPEAN REEFERS

In the two decades or so from the end of World War Two, large numbers of pure reefers were built in Western Europe, particularly by Scandinavian and West German shipyards for domestic owners.

Many of these beautifully proportioned and, with their white hulls, often yacht-like vessels, rank among the most attractive merchant ships ever built. The longest chapter in this book is devoted unashamedly to a representative selection of these *kjoleskip*, *kuhlschiffe*, and *bananiers*. Other reefers of this era are also looked at in the chapters on Salen, Lauritzen, Great White Fleet, and Geest.

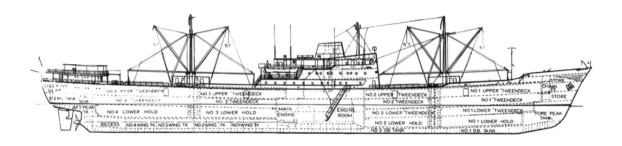

Hidlefjord -- Skips A/S Hidlefjord & Skibs A/S Byfjord (Kornelius Olsen), Norway; Akers, Oslo, 1960; 5788gt, 5233dwt, 133m, 4ha, 8x5tn der, 7900bhp Akers-B&W, 18kn. *(The Motor Ship)*

The lines of a typical handsome fruitship of this era, the Norwegian *Hidlefjord* of Kornelius Olsen. This 18kn ship and her sister *Byfjord* were both delivered in 1960 to the Stavanger owner, and were notable at the time for having B&W's first 10-cylinder opposed-piston turbocharged engines. The two forward holds had two tween decks and the two aft holds one, with the hatches all 8.2m x 4.8m. Freon 12 was used as the refrigerant and three compressors could bring cargo temperatures down to minus 18deg C. The compartments had banana bins, and sidedoors port and starboard at second deck level for each hold. Other features were unstayed tripod masts and pontoon hatch covers.

Mosdale -- **A/S Mosvold Shipping Co, Norway; Burmeister & Wain, Copenhagen, 1939; 3022gt, 2450dwt, 102m, 3400bhp B&W, 16kn. (World Ship Society)**

Scandinavian countries have always had a dominating presence in reefer shipping. Here are some of their classic reefers of an earlier era. Mosvold's *Mosdale* of 1939 was one of about eight similar ships from Burmeister & Wain, and later traded for Blue Star/Lamport & Holt and Booth Line as the *Albion Star*, *Balzac*, *Carroll*, *Norman Star* and *Basil*. She went to the breakers in 1973.

Wan Chun -- **Wan Lung Navigation Co SA, Panama; Kockums, Malmo, 1945; 3261gt, 4200dwt, 117m, 4ha, 2x2tn cr, 2x5tn, 6x3tn, 2x2tn der, 6000bhp Kockums-MAN, 17kn. (APN)**

End of the line for one of the first Norwegian-owned reefers to enter service after the war, the 3261gt *Wan Chun*, aground at IJmuiden, Holland, in November 1972 after dragging her anchors in a storm. She was launched in 1940 in Sweden as the *Pacific Express* for Oslo owner Biorn Biornstad but not delivered until September 1945. She was sold in 1963 to another Norwegian owner, Erling Hansen of Kristiansand, as the *Ranada*, and then to Chinese owners the month before her loss.

Golden Ocean -- **Trelleborgs Angfartygs A/B (Jarl Malmros), Sweden; Eriksbergs, Gothenburg, 1948; 3817gt, 4110dwt, 120m, Eriksbergs-B&W, 17.5kn. (World Ship Society)**

Two notable reefers of the immediate postwar era: The *Golden Ocean* of 1948 (above) and the *Barbara Brovig* of 1950 (below), both single screw motorships. The *Golden Ocean*, with two small cranes to serve No.2 hatch as well as a complement of derricks, was one of three very similar Swedish ships and the *Barbara Brovig*, resplendent with a typically ornate Norwegian bow emblem of this era, was the last of a trio of Belgian-built sisters for Norwegian owner Th.Brovig of Farsund.

Barbara Brovig -- **Partrederiet Brovigtank (Th. Brovig), Norway; John Cockerill, Hoboken; 1950; 3129gt, 2676dwt, 103m, Cockerill-B&W, 16.5kn. (World Ship Society)**

Samos Sea **-- Ionian Beach Marine Inc (Soutos (Hellas) Maritime Corp), Greece; Framnaes, Sandefjord, 1965; 5687gt, 6188dwt, 128m, 5ho, 4ha, 8x5tn der, 8400bhp Sulzer, 19kn. (Tolerton)**

Samos Sun **-- Fontana Shipping Inc (Soutos (Hellas) Maritime Corp), Eriksbergs, Gothenburg, 1961, 6651gt, 8397dwt, 149m, 5ha, 3x3tn cr, 1x25 & 10x5 der, 10,000bhp Eriksbergs-B&W, 18.5kn. (Tolerton)**

Two ex-Scandinavian reefers of the 60s in later service for Piraeus operator Soutos (Hellas) Maritime -- the *Samos Sea* of 1965 and the *Samos Sun* of 1961. The *Samos Sea* was originally the *Golar Fruit* of Norwegian owner Gotaas-Larsen, who had fruitships as well as tankers, and was sold in 1977. Seen in Hamburg-Sud colours, she was scrapped in 1991 at Gadani Beach as the *Amber Star*. The *Samos Sun* was built as the *Lake Eyre* for the Brostrom company A/B Tirfing, and bought by Soutos in 1975. She had three cranes as well as 11 derricks and could carry four passengers. This ship was seriously damaged in a fire at Port of Spain in July 1983 and was towed out of the harbour, beached, and abandoned as a constructive total loss.

Langstone -- **Shaw Savill & Albion Co, UK; Valmet, Helsinki, 1958; 3441gt, 3485dwt, 123m, 4ha, 8x3tn der, 6250bhp Gotaverken, 17kn. (Tolerton)**

The Finnish-built Langstone of 1958 was an interesting little reefer. Built as the Saracen, she and her sister Crusader were laid down for Swedish owner G Thorden but taken over by Crusader Shipping Co (a joint venture of Shaw Savill, New Zealand Shipping, Port, and Blue Star) to develop refrigerated trades from New Zealand to Japan, the Far East, and the US west coast in the late 50s. The Saracen was bought outright by Shaw Savill in 1971 and received the historic sailing ship name Langstone -- although her crew quickly dubbed her "the little green pig" for her seakeeping qualities. Her service was not confined to the Crusader runs -- an officer who joined her in 1973 recalls his four months aboard took in Australia-USSR (with meat), Japan-El Salvador (cars), Panama-USA (bananas), and Central America-Europe (bananas). As the Dimitrios K she was scrapped in 1981.

Aegean Reefer -- **National Ability Compania Naviera (Comninos Bros), Greece; Eriksbergs, Gothenburg, 1964; 6482/7995gt, 8525dwt, 149m, 4ha, 4x5tn cr, 10,000bhp Eriksbergs-B&W, 19kn. (Tolerton)**

Two views of the *Aegean Reefer* of 1964, a slightly undergeared-looking vessel with her four 5tn cranes. Built by Eriksbergs as the *Albany* for the Rederiet for ms Albany managed by Per Carlsson, she was a sister of the later Salen A class boats and presumably built for a long term Salen charter. In 1978 she was acquired as the *Aegean Reefer* by Comninos Brothers of Piraeus, who became the largest Greek reefer operator at this time, buying up ships West European owners were disposing of. Pictured with Lauritzen-Peninsular Reefers red and white funnel, she later traded as the *Mare I*, *Reefer Rio*, and *Itajai Reefer*, going to shipbreakers at Alang under the latter name in 1993.

Asteri -- **Afromar Inc (Soc de Gestion EVGE), Greece; Blohm & Voss, Hamburg, 1965; 6200gt, 6300dwt, 137m, 5ha, 2x5tn cr, 10x5tn der, 9600bhp MAN, 20kn. (Tolerton)**

Another Nordic beauty with a Mediterranean tan. The Greek *Asteri* was previously the *Hood River Valley* of Sweden's Johnson Line, many of whose vessels trading to the north Pacific and South America had some refrigerated capacity. However, in the 1960s the company commissioned the pure reefers *Yakima Valley* (1963) and *Rio Negro Valley* (1964) from Lindholmens, *Hood River Valley* and *Okanagan Valley* (1966) from Blohm & Voss and the larger *San Joaquin Valley* and *Aconcagua Valley* (both 1968) from Wartsila. The *Hood River Valley* and her sister were sold to Greek owners in 1971 for US$2.2m each and both scrapped in 1985.

Belnippon -- **Belships Co Skibs A/S (Christen Smith), Norway; Oresundsvarvet, Landskrona, 1964; 6313gt, 6150dwt, 138m, 4ha, 8x5tn der, 9700bhp Gotaverken, 19kn. (Tolerton)**

The *Belnippon* was among many completions from Swedish yards for Norwegian owners in the 1960s. Owned by Christen Smith of Oslo, she was sold to East Germany in 1973 and became the *John Brinckman*, going to Alang in 1993 as the *Minoan Reefer*.

Dragor Maersk -- **A/S D/S Svendborg, D/S af 1912 A/S & A P Moller, Denmark; Odense Staalskibs, 1961; 4722gt, 5550dwt, 132m, 4ha, 8x5tn der, 8100bhp B&W, 17.5kn. (Tolerton)**

Danish giant A P Moller, so prominent in every other sphere of shipping, had only a very modest involvement with pure reefers. Its first post-war was the *Dragor Maersk* of 1961 from its own Odense yard. This 17.5kn reefer was sold to Mediteranska Plovidba of Korcula in 1975 as the *Voce* and arrived at Chittagong in 1988 for demolition. In 1964 Moller added the larger 20.5kn *Thuro Maersk* and *Magleby Maersk*, both, like the *Dragor Maersk*, chartered to Salen. The *Magleby Maersk* was sold as the *Pacific Ocean* in 1976 and then three years later to Naviera del Pacifico, the shipping arm of Ecuadorian banana company Noboa, as the splendidly named *Provincia de El Oro*, now operating with an orange hull and blue funnel instead of the sky blue Maersk livery. She went to Alang in 1994.

Provincia de El Oro -- **Naviera del Pacifico SA, Ecuador; Odense Staalskibsvaerft, Odense, 1964; 6219/8222gt, 8154dwt, 148m, 4ha, 8x5th der, 13,200bhp B&W, 20.5kn. (Tolerton)**

Pacific Express -- **Sigurd Herlofson & Co, Norway; A/S Fredriksstad M/V, Fredrikstad, 1964; 6310gt, 6150dwt, 138m, 4ha, 8x5tn der, 9700bhp Gotaverken, 19.5kn. (Tolerton)**

The *Pacific Express* was completed in 1964 for Oslo owner Sigurd Herlofson. A sister to the *Belnippon* pictured earlier, like the *Belnippon* she was sold in 1973 to VEB Deutfracht as the *Fritz Reuter* when the East Germans were expanding their reefer fleet for a growing consumer society. After later trading as the Panamanian *Hawk* she arrived at Alang in 1993.

Padova Star -- **Blue Star Line, UK; Deutsche Werft, Hamburg, 1956; 2659gt, 2765dwt, 119m, 4ha, 8x5tn der, 4670bhp MAN, 16.5kn. (World Ship Society)**

An attractive little German-built reefer which saw service under three West European flags was the *Padova Star* of 1956. Built for F Laeisz as the *Parthenon*, she became Blue Star's *Padova Star* in 1964, and was sold to Italian owners two years later as the *Calarossa*. Her sister followed the same career path as *Piraus*, *Barcelona Star*, and *Calasetta*, and both saw further service with other owners before going to the breakers in 1980 and 1981 respectively.

Brunstal -- **W Bruns & Co, West Germany; Verschure & Co., Amsterdam, 1959; 2822gt, 2953dwt, 115m, 4ha, 8x5tn der, 5200bhp MAN, 17kn. (World Ship Society)**

Germany owners operated many of the most handsome reefer ships, and W Bruns & Co of Hamburg is indelibly associated with the era of the classic ships of this type. Part of a large fruit importing group, Bruns took delivery of its first new ships, *Quartole* and *Quadrivium*, in 1952. The *Brunstal* of 1959 (above) was one of two sisters bought from Torvald Klaveness, for whom she'd been the *Baleares*, in 1966. The *Brunshausen* of 1968 (below) was one of a class of fifteen 4700gt, 136m, fast 21kn ships for which the Bruns fleet is probably best remembered. All could carry passengers -- most of them 12.

Brunshausen -- **Partenreederi ms 'Brunshausen' (W Bruns & Co), West Germany; Howaldtswerke, Hamburg, 1968; 3201/4623gt, 5300dwt, 136m, 4ha, 1x10tn & 7x5tn der, 10,500bhp MAN, 21kn. (World Ship Soc.)**

Brunsbuttel -- Partenreederei ms 'Brunsbuttel' (W Bruns & Co), West Germany; Howaldtswerke, Hamburg, 1968; 3201/4623gt, 5300dwt, 136m, 4ha, 1x10 & 7x5tn der, 10,500bhp MAN, 21kn. (World Ship Society)

Two more completions to this design were the *Brunsbuttel* of 1968 (above) and *Brunsland* of 1964 (below). The ships were designed for Bruns by Blohm & Voss which built three including the first, the *Brunshausen* of 1963, which was sold to the USSR three years later. Other completions came from Howaldtswerke (four), Lubecker Flenderwerke (six), and Rheinstahl Nordseewerke (two). Rheinstahl also completed six ships to this design in 1964 for the Soviet Union, which also later purchased another four from Bruns. Another was built for Harald Schuldt of Hamburg by Howaldtswerke, bringing total completions to the design to 22.

Brunsland -- Partenreederei ms 'Brunsland' (W Bruns & Co), West Germany; Blohm & Voss, Hamburg, 1964; 3372/4697gt, 4152dwt, 136m, 4ha, 1x10 & 7x5tn der, 9600bhp MAN, 21kn. (World Ship Society)

Benadir – **Soc Siciliana Servizi Marittima SpA, Italy; 4767gt. (World Ship Society)**

Apart from the first two sold to the USSR in 1966-67, the ships of this class were disposed of by Bruns in 1971 to 1978. Pictured later in their careers are the *Benadir* (above), the former *Brunsland* of 1964 pictured on the previous page, and, still in Bruns funnel colours, the *Elita*, ex-*Brunseck* of 1964. The well-raked stem, large mast houses for the cooling machinery, and accommodation house inset at weather deck level – all characteristic of this design – are apparent. Bruns disappeared from shipowning after owner Astheimer was bought by Castle & Cooke (Dole) in 1976, their last ships all getting Castle & Cooke "Tropical" names in 1978.

Elita – **Martropico Armadora, Greece; Lubecker Flenderwerke, Lubeck, 1964; 3272/4618gt, 5132dwt, 135m, 4ha, 1x10tn & 7x5tn der, 9600bhp MAN, 20kn. (World Ship Society)**

Pacific Fruit -- **Great South East Lines, Singapore; Blohm & Voss, Hamburg, 1964; 3279/4628gt, 5129dwt, 136m, 4ha, 1x10tn & 7x5tn der, 9600bhp Blohm & Voss-MAN, 21kn. (Tolerton)**

Another of the Bruns reefers later in her career. The Singapore-owned *Pacific Fruit* had been the *Brunsholm* of 1964, and after being sold in 1972 traded as the *Lily*, *Ronirel*, *Pacific Fruit*, and *Comfort* before going to the breakers at Kaohsiung in 1984.

Minden -- **Elmina Shipping Co (Enterprises Shipping & Trading), Greece; Rickmers, Bremerhaven, 1964; 4626gt, 6515dwt, 143m, 4ha, 8x5tn der, 9800bhp Borsig, 20kn. (Tolerton)**

Contrary to what the Greek lettering on her stern suggests, the *Minden* of 1964 retained the same name during service with both Scipio & Co of Bremen and, after her sale in 1980, Restis's Enterprises Shipping & Trading of Piraeus. She was scrapped at Gadani Beach in 1985 as the Honduran *Milos IV*.

Persimmon - Partenreederei ms Persimmon (F Laeisz), West Germany; Deutsche Werft, Hamburg, 1967; 3428/4914gt, 6560dwt, 139m, 4ha, 1x3-8tn & 7x3-5tn der, 11,400bhp MAN, 22kn. (Tolerton)

Plod - Mediteranska Plovidba, Yugoslavia; Deutsche Werft, Hamburg, 1960; 3415/4747gt, 4299dwt, 134m, 4ha, 7250bhp MAN, 18.5kn. (Tolerton)

The reefers of F Laeisz of Hamburg were worthy successors to the famous sailing ships of Laeisz's "Flying P" fleet, and made up one of the biggest German reefer fleets. Laeisz's involvement with reefers went back to the *Pungo* and *Pioner*, both completed with unfortunate timing in 1914 on the eve of war, for the fruit trade with German African colonies. In the 1950s and 60s Laeisz took delivery of 20 or so reefers including the trio on this page. More than half were built by Deutsche Werft, Hamburg, including the 22kn *Persimmon* of 1967 (top), one of four very fast banana carriers, and the *Pentelikon* of 1960 seen (centre) after being sold in 1974 to the Yugoslav operator Mediteranska Plovidba as the inappropriately named *Plod*. The *Portunus* of 1955 (bottom) was a completion of Kieler Howaldtswerke and is seen later in her career as the Singaporean *Orchard Gold*. She was scrapped at Kaohsiung in 1980, while the *Persimmon* was broken up at Lisbon in 1985 as the *Grand United* and the *Plod* went to Gadani Beach in 1986.

Orchard Gold – Pacific Gold Shipping, Singapore; Kieler Howaldtswerke, Kiel, 1955; 4257gt, 125m, 4ha, 8x5tn der, 5140bhp MAN, 17kn. (Kevin Moore collection)

Ice Pilot -- **Othoca Shipping Corp (United Sea Services), Greece; Deutsche Werft, Hamburg, 1964; 3838/5294gt, 5693dwt, 141m, 4ha, 1x10tn & 7x5tn der, 9600bhp MAN, 21kn. (Tolerton)**

The *Pisang* of 1964 was another Deutsche Werft completion. She became the *Frostfjord* in 1971 and was sold to Greek owners in 1979 as the *Ice Pilot* (above). One of three fast 2lkn banana carriers for Laeisz, she was a forerunner of the *Persimmon* type and could carry 12 passengers. Laeisz's involvement with reefers included the 22kn Belgian-built and flagged (thanks to extremely cheap government shipbuilding finance) trio of the *Pocantico*, *Potomac*, and *Pocahontas* (below) of 1979-80. Presumably not coincidental with their American names, all three saw extensive service with United Brands, and the *Pocahontas* is pictured in the American company's funnel colours. She had side doors port and starboard for all four holds, and could carry 114 containers on deck. Cargo could be carried at down to minus 25deg C in three holds forward and one aft.

Pocahontas -- **Ahlers NV, Belgium; Boelwerf, Tamise, 1980; 7095gt, 9852dwt, 151m, 4ha, 4x5tn cr, 16,520bhp MAN, 22kn. (Tolerton)**

Polar Ecuador **-- Hamburg-Sudamerikanische Dampfschifffahrts-Gesellschaft Eggert & Amsinck, West Germany; Blohm & Voss, Hamburg, 1967; 3815/5617gt, 7832dwt, 147m, 4ha, 8x5tn der, 14,880bhp 2 x Pielstick, 22.5kn. (World Ship Society)**

Among the most dramatic looking reefers were Hamburg-Sud's *Polar Ecuador (1967)*, *Polar Argentina*, *Polar Colombia*, *Polar Brasil*, *Polar Uruguay*, and *Polar Paraguay* (1968). Built by Blohm & Voss, these 5600gt, 22kn twin-engined, single screw ships were a little larger than contemporary German reefers and suitable for both banana and meat carriage. They had two 5tn derricks at each hatch, with one pair stepped from the sweeping funnels, and transom stern. All were initially chartered to Salen.

Polar Uruguay **-- Hamburg-Sudamerikanische Dampfschifffahrts-Gesellschaft Eggert & Amsinck, West Germany; Blohm & Voss, Hamburg, 1968; 3834/5636gt, 7832dwt, 147m, 4ha, 8x5tn der, 14,880bhp 2 x Pielstick, 23.5kn. (World Ship Society)**

Lola -- **Dawn Flight Marine Co, Cyprus; 3840/5644gt, 7896dwt. (Kevin Moore collection)**

Two of the class under later Cypriot ownership: The grace of these vessels was little diminished when the *Polar Uruguay* was operating under her fifth name as the *Lola* (above) after previously trading as the *Aegean Bay*, *Frio Bay*, and *Frio Bahia*. *Lola* went to Alang in 1993. Also on her fifth name which she took to Alang in 1998 after a similar progression of owners was the *Miramar* (below), built as the *Polar Colombia* before becoming the *Aegean Progress*, *Frio Progress*, and *Frio Venezuela*.

Miramar -- **Garden Venus Shipping Co, Cyprus; Blohm & Voss, Hamburg, 1968; 3827/5631gt, 7949dwt, 147m, 4ha, 8x5tn der, 14,880bhp 2 x Pielstick, 22kn. (Kevin Moore collection)**

Polar Honduras -- Hamburg-Sudamerikanische Dampfschiff-Ges.Eggert & Amsinck (Rudolf A Oetker), West Germany; Flender Werft, Lubeck, 1979; 6970/9996gt, 10,873dwt, 154m, 4ha, 8x3-5tn der, 18,660bhp MAN, 22kn. (Tolerton)

More austere-looking additions to the Hamburg-Sud fleet but still handsome ships were the *Polar Honduras* (above) and *Polar Costa Rica* (below), completed in 1979 at Lubeck. The pair were later editions of P&O's *Wild Cormorant* and *Wild Curlew,* and both were sold via Union-Castle for Universal Reefers service in 1981 but reverted to their original names in 1994 for Nassau owners. The *Polar Costa Rica* is pictured in this phase of her career, still obviously operating for Hamburg-Sud.

Polar Costa Rica -- Daffodil Maritime (Lagoa Shipping Corp), Bahamas; Flender Werft, Lubeck, 1979; 6970/9996gt, 10,870dwt, 154m, 4ha, 8x3-5tn der, 16,169bhp MAN, 21kn. (Tolerton)

Marko Polo -- **Mediteranska Plovidba, Yugoslavia; Kieler Howaldtswerke, Kiel, 1958; 3158/4071gt, 2982dwt, 126m, 4ha, 1x10 & 7x5tn der, 6000bhp MAN, 17kn. (Tolerton)**

The classic lines of an earlier generation of Hamburg-Sud reefers -- the *Cap Domingo* of 1958 under later Yugoslav ownership as Mediteranska Plovidba's *Marko Polo*. Hamburg-Sud's first pure reefer, she was sold in 1970 to become the Bergen Line's *Crux* for the Norwegian-South America Line service, and sold to the Yugoslavs three years later. She was broken up at Split in 1985.

Luhesand -- **Partenreederei ms Luhesand (A F Harmstorf & Co), West Germany; Schlichting Werft, Travemunde, 1967; 1673gt, 1947dwt, 88m, 3ha, 6x3tn der, 2750bhp Atlas, 16kn. (Tolerton)**

Hamburg owner A Harmstorf operated a number of small reefers in the 60s and 70s like the *Luhesand*, pictured far from home in a New Zealand port. All were built at Travemunde by Schlichting Werft.

Fort Dauphin -- **Cie Generale Transatlantique, France; Alex Stephen, Glasgow, 1949; 5038gt, 4059dwt, 122m, 5600bhp 2 x Stephen-Sulzer, 16kn. (Keith Byass)**

It's no surprise that France, with a tradition of handsome ships and pride in aesthetics, numbered some beautiful reefers in its merchant fleet. Among them were the Cie Generale Transatlantique's twin-engined *Fort Dauphin* of 1949 (above), one of a 16kn trio of which A Stephen & Sons contributed this vessel and the *Fort Richepanse* and Ateliers & Chantiers de Provence the *Fort Richelieu*, and the *Fort Carillon* of 1953 (below), one of a pair of more streamlined single-engined 16.5kn French-built vessels with her sister *Fort Desaix*.

Fort Carillon -- **Cie Generale Transatlantique, France; Atel & Ch de Bretagne, Nantes, 1953; 4887gt, 3257dwt, 112m, 6000bhp B&W, 16.5kn. (World Ship Society)**

Rainbow Star -- **Cazalet Investments Corp (Chartworld Shipping), Liberia; Cons Nav & Ind de la Mediterranee, La Seyne, 1969; 9716gt, 8640dwt, 146m, 5ha, 1x20, 9x5, 2x3tn der, 16,740bhp 2 x Pielstick, 20.5kn. (Wim Plokker)**

A poorer advertisement for French design was a later CGT reefer, the utilitarian *Fort Pontchartrain* of 1969, seen under later ownership and her fourth name as the *Rainbow Star*. She had one sister, the *Fort La Reine* of 1969, which carried a record banana cargo to Rouen on her maiden voyage. They were both sold by what had now evolved into Cie Generale Maritime to Flamar Interocean of Panama in 1980.

Frysna -- **Fathom Fisheries (Tonga) Ltd, Tonga; At Duchesne & Bossiere, Le Havre, 1964; 298gt, 495dwt, 57m, 2ha, 4x2tn der, 890bhp MAN. (Tolerton)**

Reefers do not come much more diminutive than the 298gt French-built *Frysna*, a well-known vessel in the South Pacific in her day. She was completed in 1964 as the *Frigomare*, one of three similar ships owned by Einar Reiss, and after being renamed *Frysna* by another Oslo owner Per Selvig in 1970 was sold to Tongan operator Peter Warner, for whom her ice-strengthening was definitely superfluous, as the *Frysna* in 1973.

Bambara -- **Cie de Navigation Fraissinet & Cyprien Fabre, France; Ch Reunis Loire-Normandie, Grand Quevilly, 1957; 4410gt, 3000dwt, 114m, 4ha, 5750bhp B&W, 18kn. (World Ship Society)**

The *Bambara* of 1957 for Cie de Navigation Fraissinet & Cyprien Fabre was one of several motorships of similar profile for these Marseilles owners, with bipod masts and No.3 hatch between the bridge and engineroom. She was rebuilt as a livestock carrier for Saudi owners in 1973 and broken up in 1986.

Karukera -- **Cie de Navigation Fruitiere, France; At & Ch de Nantes (Bretagne-Loire), Nantes, 1963; 5402gt, 4580dwt, 120m, 4ha, 8x5tn der, 8400bhp B&W, 18.25kn. (Tolerton)**

The flush-decked *Karukera* of 1963 with two bipod masts and capacity for 10 passengers was the last of a quartet of broadly similar fruitships with three holds forward and one aft built for Cie de Navigation Fruitiere of Paris.

San Nicolas -- **Fenrich Investment Inc (Ost-West-Handel), Cambodia; At & Ch de Dunkerque & Bordeaux (France-Gironde), Dunkirk, 1969; 8610gt, 6625dwt, 144m, 4ha, 4x5tn cr, 13,860bhp B&W, 20kn. (Kees Lous)**

The French apogee came with a class of eight 8500gt, 20kn ships from Ateliers & Chantiers de Dunkerque & Bordeaux (France-Gironde) at Dunkirk for various companies including Messageries Maritimes, Chargeurs Reunis, and Cie Generale Transatlantique -- the *Narval* and *Aquilon* of 1968, *Belouga, Fribourg, Marsouin, Ivondro, Favorita,* and *Fort Sainte Marie* of 1969. The *San Nicolas* (above) was originally the *Marsouin* of Courtage & Transports, Paris, and went to Alang in 1999. Cie de Navigation Fruitiere's *Belouga* (below), chartered to Lauritzen, is pictured sharing a wharf with Lauritzen's *Nippon Reefer* at a New Zealand port in a now historic view, loading meat from insulated rail wagons.

Belouga -- **Cie de Navigation Fruitiere, France; France-Gironde, Dunkirk, 1969; 4413/8554gt, 6490dwt, 144m, 4ha, 4x5tn cr, 13,860bhp B&W, 20.5kn. (Tolerton)**

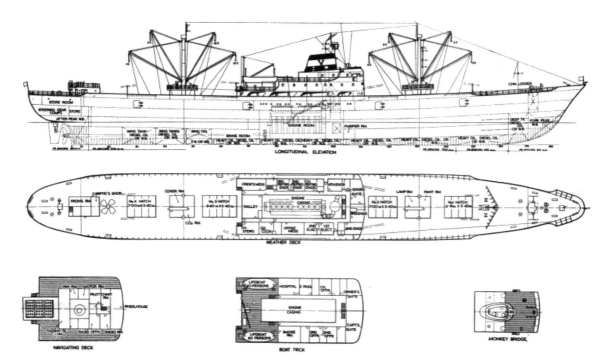

Ondine -- **Caribbean Atlantic Cargo Inc, Panama; Ch Nav des Flandres, Bruges, 1960; 5960gt, 4433dwt, 139m, 4ha, 2x10tn & 6x5tn der, 7200bhp MAN, 19kn. (*The Motor Ship*)**

Belgian shipbuilder Chantiers Navals des Flandres contributed another of the many smart-looking reefer designs of the early 1960s with the banana carrier *Ondine* of 1960.

Built for a Panamanian company for a 15-year charter to Standard Fruit of New Orleans to carry bananas from Central America, the *Ondine* was the first of three reefers from the Bruges yard, followed by *Orpheus* (1961) and Scipio & Co's *Elsfleth* which is illustrated in the frontispiece to this chapter.

However, while the *Ondine* had two sets of samson posts and MAN machinery, the *Elsfleth* -- also built against a 15-year Standard Fruit charter -- had conventional pole masts and a turbocharged Borsig-Fiat engine.

The four holds of the *Ondine* divided into 14 main compartments, subdivided again into banana bins by wooden battens, and could be cooled down to minus 12deg C.

One technical journal was unhappy about the new vessel's crew accommodation. It deemed it "of a needlessly high standard and expense."

The V on the funnel of the *Ondine* stands for Vaccaro, the New Orleans Sicilian family who started importing bananas from Honduras at the end of the 19th century and established Standard Fruit and Steamship Corporation in 1926.

At the time the *Ondine* came into service, Standard Fruit had just started importing the new Cavendish variety which did not transport well in bins, and was pioneering an expensive transition from shipping bananas in bunches to instead shipping them in corrugated cardboard boxes.

Standard Fruit ranked second only to the giant United Fruit in the US banana trade, but it was struggling financially and in the mid-1960s Castle & Cooke (Dole), the Hawaiian pineapple giant, acquired the company in an amicable takeover.

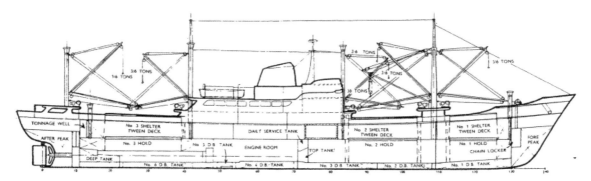

Velazquez -- **MacAndrews & Co, UK; Nobiskrug Werft, Rendsburg, 1954; 2196gt, 2527dwt, 101m, 3ha, 1x30, 10 x 6tn der, 2xMAN, 15.75kn. (*The Motor Ship*)**

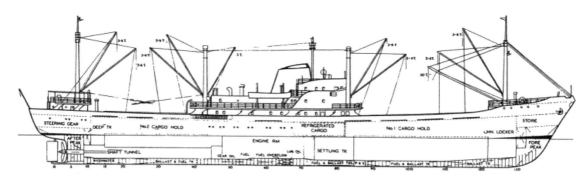

Velarde -- **MacAndrews & Co, UK; Ottensener, Hamburg, 1957; 2055gt, 101m, 2ha, 3800bhp 2xMAN, 15.5kn. (*The Motor Ship*)**

It might stretch the parameters of this book but it would be inappropriate not to include a mention in this chapter of the fruitships of MacAndrews and Co, which with their white hulls, neat lines, and prominent involvement in the Mediterranean fruit trade were no doubt often mistaken for pure reefers. The fruitship *Velazquez* of 1954 (top) from Nobiskrug was the first of two 2200gt vessels in one of the earliest British postwar orders from a German yard, and had three large mechanically ventilated holds designed for fruit cargoes. She also carried 12 passengers. MacAndrews also went to Germany for the 2055gt *Velarde* (centre) of 1957 designed for the Spanish fruit trade and with two long holds (again mechanically ventilated), plus two refrigerated compartments aft of No.1 hold. Both the *Velazquez* and *Velarde* were twin-engined single screw vessels with similar MAN machinery. The *Verdaguer* of 1958 (right, at Algeciras on her maiden voyage) was one of the pair from Krogerwerft. Bruce Carr, a young 2nd engineer who stood by during construction in Rendsburg, recalls a maiden voyage -- after Baltic trials and passage through the Kiel canal -- taking in London, Bilbao, Cadiz, Seville, Algeciras, Alicante, Almeria, Lisbon, Porto, Southampton, and back to London.

Verdaguer -- **MacAndrews & Co, UK; Krogerwerft, Rendsburg, 1958; 2049gt, 101m, 3ha, 3800bhp 2xMAN, 15.5kn. (Bruce Carr)**

Fastelle -- **Fastelle Shipping Co (Whitwill, Cole), Hong Kong; Scotstoun Marine, Scotstoun, 1975; 8043/10,396gt, 11,167dwt, 157m, 5ha, 4x12.5tn cr, 2x8tn der, 18,800bhp Kincaid-B&W, 21.5kn. (Tolerton)**

Aside from the tonnage for companies like Blue Star and Geest dealt with elsewhere in this book, the best of British in this era included the two Loch class ships for Denholm (above) and British & Commonwealth's R class Clan Line quartet (opposite page).

The *Loch Lomond* of 1975 -- pictured later in her career as the Hong Kong-registered *Fastelle* -- and the *Loch Maree* of 1976, along with the older ex-Brostrom vessel *Loch Long*, were Denholm's first excursion into reefer management as tramp operators like it diversified. Described as "sports cars of the sea" by one master, the Clyde-built Lochs were extremely popular ships with their crews. During six years service with Denholm the *Loch Lomond* primarily operated on three runs -- bananas from Puerto Limon to Europe and from Central America (Puerto Limon, Golfito, Armuelles, Puerto Bolivar) to Los Angeles, and citrus from Los Angeles to Japan and Hong Kong, making Los Angeles something of a home port. The design was the first created by Govan Shipbuilders after the Upper Clyde Shipbuilders collapse. After a career under eight names, she arrived at Alang in 2000 for demolition.

Designed as fruitships for the South African trade, the *Clan Ramsay* class (opposite) from Greenock Dockyard had a small uninsulated space in the forecastle tweendeck. Usually laid up at Southampton off-season, they were handsome ships in spite of the absence of sheer which enhanced the grace of slightly earlier reefers.

Clan Ranald -- Union-Castle Mail SS Co (Cayzer, Irvine & Co), UK; Greenock Dockyard, Greenock, 1965; 7955gt, 11,730dwt, 161m, 5ha, 2x5.5tn & 8x5tn der, 10,350bhp Kincaid-B&W, 17.5kn. (Trevor Jones)

The *Clan Ramsay*, *Clan Ranald* (above), and *Clan Robertson* were completed in 1965, and the *Clan Ross* in 1966. They were renamed in 1976 and 1977 becoming respectively the *Winchester Castle*, *Dover Castle*, *Balmoral Castle*, and *Kinpurnie Castle*. In 1979 for Universal Reefers, a Safmarine and Union-Castle joint venture, the Castle suffixes were replaced by Universal. In the early 80s all were sold to Greek owners. The first to go was the class's lead ship *Winchester Universal* (ex-*Clan Ramsay*) which became Kappa Maritime's *Lady Madonna* in 1980. She is pictured (below) at the New Zealand port of Timaru in December that year loading a cargo of meat for Iran. None of the four exceeded 20 years in service, and the *Lady Madonna* arrived at Gadani Beach in 1985.

Lady Madonna -- Braganza Bay Shipping Corp (Kappa Maritime), Greece; Greenock Dockyard, Greenock, 1965; 7952gt, 11,918dwt, 161m, 5ha, 2x5.5tn & 8x5tn der, 10,350bhp Kincaid-B&W, 17.5kn. (Tolerton)

Mare Boreale -- 'Oriens' Societa di Navigazione per Azione (Fratelli d'Amico), Italy; Italcantieri, Spezia, 1967; 6952gt, 5690dwt, 142m, 4ha, 8x5tn der, 10,800bhp Ansaldo-B&W, 19.5kn. (Tolerton)

As you'd expect, there's a touch of chic about the Italian-built reefers of this period. It's visible in the lines of the *Mare Boreale* of 1967, one of four 6950gt, 19kn Palermo-registered sisters from Italcantieri and Ansaldo for Fratelli d'Amico, and even in a class of five ships for the Soviet Union -- 4000gt, 19kn ships from Breda like the *Sergey Lazo* of 1968 (below). Others of this class were the *Chapayev* of 1967, the *Kotovskiy* and *Parkhomenko* of 1968, and the *Nikolay Shchors* of 1969. The *Sergey Lazo* went to Alang breakers as *Liza* in 1999, and the *Mare Boreale* to Chittagong in 1994 as the *Banana Trader*.

Sergey Lazo -- Black Sea Shipping Co, USSR; Cant Nav Breda, Venice, 1968; 4059gt, 4562dwt, 121m, 4ha (2ho), 8x3tn der, 7600bhp Fiat, 19kn. (Tolerton)

Rio Amazonas -- **Flota Bananera Ecuatoriana, Ecuador; Cant Nav Apuania, Carrara, 1968; 6625gt, 5598dwt, 139m, 4ha, 8x5tn der, 1x5tn cr, 10,500bhp Fiat, 20kn. (Tolerton)**

That Italian elegant touch was also apparent in the 6625gt 1968 sisters *Rio Amazonas* and *Islas Galapagos* from the Apuania shipyard, both built for Ecuadorian state company Flota Bananera Ecuatoriana (liquidated in 1987) and later part of Luis Noboa's Naviera del Pacifico without change of name. The former went to Chittagong breakers in 1997 and the *Islas Galapagos* to Alang in 1994.

Islas Galapagos -- **Flota Bananera Ecuatoriana, Ecuador; Cant Nav Apuania, Carrara, 1968; 6625gt, 5598dwt, 139m, 4ha, 8x5tn der, 1x5tn cr, 10,500bhp Fiat, 20kn. (Tolerton)**

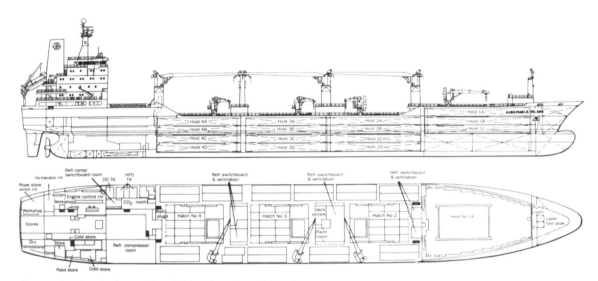

Albemarle Island of 1993, lead ship of a class of five for the Noboa group of Ecuador. (*The Motor Ship*)

Barrington Island -- K/S Difko LXXXII (Ecuadorian Line), Bahamas; Danyard, Frederikshavn, 1993; 14,061gt,14,140dwt, 178m, 4ha, 3x40tn & 4x10tn cr, 22,187bhp Mitsui-B&W, 21.5kn. (David Salisbury/ Trevor Jones collection)

CHAPTER THREE
MODERN WESTERN EUROPEAN-BUILT REEFERS

While in most spheres of shipbuilding Western European yards have struggled to compete with Far Eastern shipbuilders in the last three decades or so, they continued to contribute reefer tonnage, and the vessels of this era are the subject of this chapter. However, some of the modern reefer classes from Western European yards are covered elsewhere in this book in the chapters covering specific companies. It's also to be noted that "modern" is a slight misnomer, for there has not been significant reefer construction in Western European yards in the current decade.

Denmark has contributed some of the most important modern refrigerated ships. A reefer milestone of the 1990s came with the introduction of five 14,000gt sisters from Danyard for the Ecuadorian Noboa group -- the *Albemarle Island* of 1993 followed by the *Barrington Island*, *Charles Island*, and *Duncan Island* (all 1993), and *Hood Island* (1994).

As well as their giant size which obviously drew on Danyard's experience with supersize reefers for Lauritzen (the "Family" class) and Chiquita and Geest, the five Noboa ships -- hailed as the "green" reefers -- are notable for using anhydrous ammonia as their primary refrigerant. Ammonia, flammable but more environmentally friendly than the standard R22 (HCFC, hydrochlorofluorocarbon) used for marine refrigeration, had not been used on a reefer for two decades before the *Albemarle Island* was built. The ship was also the first to have Lloyd's Register's special notation for controlled atmosphere operation.

The cargo spaces can be cooled to minus 29deg C, and two air coolers and fans in each of the 15 cargo compartments can effect the up to 90 air changes an hour required for banana cargoes. The ships have three 40tn electro-hydraulic cranes for container or pallet handling plus four 10tn cranes, offset to the starboard side, for pallet handling through small hatches in the main hatch covers. The ships were designed to carry 434 TEU containers, 112 in the holds and 322 (including 148 refrigerated) on deck, as well as pallets and break bulk cargo.

Akademikis Zavarickis -- **Ringmare Shipping Co (Latmar Columbia (Cyprus)), Cyprus; Aalborg Vaerft, Aalborg, 1986; 9552gt, 7673dwt, 138m, 4ha, 4x8tn cr, 13,051bhp Bryansk-B&W, 20kn. (Tolerton)**

In 1985-86 Aalborg Vaerft completed the *Akademik N Vavilov*, *Akademik Zavaritskiy*, and *Skulptor Tomskiy*, three 9500gt, 20kn reefers that set a new standard for reefers in the Soviet merchant fleet. After the Soviet breakup they hoisted the Latvian flag in 1991 as part of the large Latvian Shipping Co fleet, with the names changing to *Akademikis Vavilovs*, *Akademikis Zavarickis*, and *Skulptors Tomskis*. The *Akademikis Vavilovs* is pictured (below) chartered to Lauritzen soon after the transition, while the *Akademikis Zavarickis* is pictured (above) a few years later, operating for Cool Carriers and -- like many former Soviet ships including her two sisters -- now registered in Cyprus.

Akademikis Vavilovs -- **Latvian Shipping Co, Latvia; Aalborg Vaerft, Aalborg, 1985; 9552gt, 7673dwt, 138m, 4ha, 4x8tn cr, 13,050bhp Bryansk-B&W, 20kn. (Tolerton)**

Frio Seattle -- **Stefanina Marine Co (Laskaridis Shipping Co), Cyprus; Aarhus Flydedok, Aarhus, 1997; 3817gt, 4000dwt, 97m, 2ha, 2x8tn cr, 4418bhp MaK, 15.5kn. (Tolerton)**

Another Danish yard, Aarhus Flydedok, built six smaller 3800gt reefers, also with a Russian connection, more recently, including the *Frio Seattle* of 1997. These ships, starting with the *Alexandra* of 1997, were flagged in the Bahamas and designed to service the Russian Pacific fishing fleet but also to operate in the fruit trades. Like other modern reefers, they are pallet-friendly and can carry 54 TEUs, and also have tanks for carrying fuel to the fishing fleet. The *Frio Seattle*, showing the efficiency of her bow thruster here, was built as the *Galaktika* but snapped up by Laskaridis in 1999.

Ice Crystal -- **Fairway Shipping A/S (Copenhagen Reefers), Denmark; Aarhus Flyedok, Aarhus, 1991; 3625gt, 3043dwt, 92m, 2ha, 2x4tn cr, 2787bhp B&W, 13.3kn. (Kees Lous)**

An earlier design from Aarhus -- the refrigerated pallets carrier *Ice Crystal* and her sisters *Ice Star* and *Ice Clipper* were built for Mortensen & Lange's Copenhagen Reefers. As well as two cranes, they have two pallet lifts serving the three cargo decks through two starboard sidedoors, and can carry 42 TEUs.

49

Ice Louise -- **Ocean T Shipping AS (Fjord Shipping AS), Norway; Frederikshavn Vaerft, Frederikshavn, 1980; 1884gt, 2225dwt, 75m, 3ha, 3x5tn der, 1860bhp B&W Alpha, 11.5kn. (Kees Lous)**

Another small Danish reefer design -- the *Ice Louise*, built as the *Pacific Governess*, was one of a series of six modest 11.5kn ships from Frederikshavn Vaerft.

Ouro Do Brasil -- **Promenade Shipping Corp, Liberia; Kvaerner Kleven Floro, Floro, 1993; 15,218gt, 18,600dwt, 173m 16ta, 16,560hp Sulzer, 20kn. (author's collection)**

Reefer or tanker? Fruit juice carriers like the *Ouro Do Brasil* are a recent marine specialisation, carrying a refrigerated cargo in bulk that reefers used to carry in drums. The first of two sisters from Norway's Kvaerner Kleven for the trade from Brazil, this ship, completed in 1993, has four holds each with four cylindrical stainless steel tanks, a small hose-handling crane, and can also carry 240 TEUs on deck.

Chilean Reefer -- K/S Chilean Reefer (Barber Ship Mgmt), Norway; Drammen Slip & Verk, Drammen, 1984; 9092gt, 11,800dwt, 149m, 4ha (3ho), 4x8tn cr, 7680bhp Mitsubishi-Sulzer, 17.75kn. (Tolerton)

The Drammen shipyard's involvement with reefers did not end with its famous standard series. Drammen owner Peter Berg, who had ordered some of the last ships of that series, followed up with orders for two 9000gt, 17.75kn ships, the *Elisabeth B* of 1984 and *Cacilia B* of 1985. Operating in the Lauritzen pool, they took JL names in 1986 as the *Chilean Reefer* and *Colombian Reefer* respectively. Both had four side doors each side.

Iran Mofid -- Islamic Republic of Iran Shipping Lines, Iran; Framnaes, Sandefjord, 1979; 6773/9073gt, 12,475dwt, 156m, 4ha, 1x10, 1x5.5, 3x5tn cr, 20,100bhp Horten-Sulzer, 22kn. (Tolerton)

Fellow Norwegian builder Framnaes, which contributed two of the Drammens, also followed up with four large reefers, the *Hilco Sprinter* and *Hilco Speedster* (both 1979), *Hilco Scamper* (1980), and *Hilco Skier* (1981), while a fifth ship, the *Hilco Skater* of 1981 was similar. Built for Irgens Larsen of Oslo, the quartet were powerful 22kn ships with provision for 135 TEUs and five sidedoors port and starboard. Fuel consumption was high -- 73tn a day. The *Speedster* took her sixth name when she became the *Iran Mofid* in 1989 and carried it to the breakers at Alang 13 years later.

Belgium's Boelwerf contributed to the modern reefer fleet with the six ships of the 7700gt, 20kn Crystal P series for F Laeisz and Cool Carriers, starting with the *Crystal Prince* and followed by the *Crystal Pride*, *Crystal Primadonna*, and *Crystal Privilege* (all 1992) and *Crystal Pilgrim* and *Crystal Pioneer* (1994). They were flagged in Luxembourg.

Configured like other modern reefers for both pallets and (on deck) containers, the three-hold Crystal ships are unusual in having hatches 2 and 3 offset to starboard, with the covers on the weather deck stowing vertically along the centreline when the hatches are open.

Another novel feature is a hydraulically operated rain shelter incorporated in each weather deck hatch cover, to permit all-weather cargo handling. The three large holds are of similar size and all with four tween decks.

In contrast to the contemporary *Albemarle Island* class, the Crystals have conventional HCFC (R22) refrigeration. Cargo can be carried at down to minus 30deg C, and they were designed to carry 68 TEUs on deck. Fuel consumption is 35tn a day.

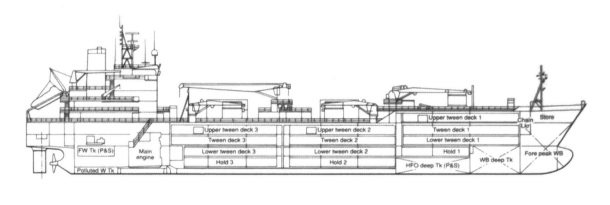

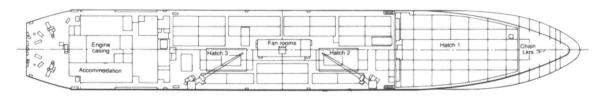

The *Crystal Pride* class from Boelwerf -- profile and main deck drawings. (*The Motor Ship*)

Crystal Privilege -- **Leif Hoegh & Co Shipping AS (Hoegh Fleet Services), Bahamas; Boelwerf, Temse, 1992; 7743gt, 7726dwt, 131m, 3ha, 1x34tn & 3x8tn cr, 11,012bhp Mitsui-B&W, 19.6kn. (Tolerton)**

The *Crystal Privilege* (above) and the *Crystal Primadonna* (below) are pictured operating in LauritzenCool colours after they and the *Crystal Prince* and *Crystal Pride* had been sold in 1996 to Leif Hoegh's International Reefer Ltd of Bermuda for US$73 million.

Crystal Primadonna -- **Leif Hoegh & Co Shipping AS (Hoegh Fleet Services), Bahamas; Boelwerf, Temse, 1992; 7743gt, 7726dwt, 131m, 3ha, 1x34tn & 3x8tn cr, 11,012bhp Mitsui-B&W, 19.6kn. (Tolerton)**

Tundra Queen **-- Kvaerner Reefer A/S (Irgens Larsen), Liberia; Astilleros Espanoles, Seville, 1991; 11,658gt, 12714dwt, 158m, 4ha, 4x19tn cr, 13,250bhp AESA-B&W, 20kn. (Tolerton)**

Spanish yards have contributed a significant portion of modern West European reefer tonnage, with a major series being the 11,600gt, 20kn ships from Astilleros Espanoles like the *Tundra Queen* of 1991. Five ships and four slightly smaller but similar vessels were built in this series for the Del Monte group, the *Tundra Queen* being completed as the *Del Monte Quality* before she and two sisters quickly swapped "Del Monte" for "Tundra" names. With a large container capacity of 362 TEUs, she has two sets of powerful twin 19tn electro-hydraulic cranes, and was designed for a crew of 16. Fuel consumption is 46tns a day.

Frost Olympos **-- Ramor International Inc (East Line Reefer Co), Russia; Astilleros Espanoles, Seville, 1980; 3835gt, 4392dwt, 103m, 4ha, 3x3tn cr, 4400bhp AESA-B&W, 15kn. (Tolerton)**

A more humble earlier series from Asterillos Espanoles was a class of eight ships like the *Frost Olympos* of 1980. Most were built for Spanish operator Compania Naviera Transmarina, the *Frost Olympos* as the *Frigo Oceania*. All but one later became part of the ubiquitous Laskaridis fleet, this vessel as the *Frio America* and then as the *Frost Olympos.*

Sierra Laurel -- **Maritima del Norte, Panama; Construcciones Navales P Freire, Vigo, 1998; 5100gt, 5937dwt, 117m, 4ha, 4x5tn cr, 6662bhp B&W, 16kn. (Tolerton)**

Another modern Spanish design -- the 5100gt *Sierra Laurel* of 1998 and her sisters *Sierra Lara*, *Sierra Leyre*, and *Sierra Loba* were 1996-98 completions from the P Freire yard, Vigo, for Maritima del Norte of Madrid, designed for fishing fleet support (for which they have two deep tanks for diesel oil), as well as general reefer trading.

Loen Stream -- **Oslo Shipholding AS (Roswell Navigation Corp), Bahamas; Astilleros del Atlantico, Santander, 1982; 2573g, 1992dwt, 74m, 2ha (1ho), 2990bhp Wartsila-Alpha, 14.5kn. (Kees Lous)**

The *Loen Stream* of 1982 is a reefer curiosity, one of four small ro-ro ships built by Astilleros del Atlantico at Santander. As well as one refrigerated cargo hold she has a stern door and ramp, a side door, and capacity for more than 200 cars.

Iberian Reefer -- **Naviera Extremena SA (Lauritzen Reefers), Spain; Astilleros del Cadagua, Bilbao, 1985; 7949gt, 10,168dwt, 134m, 4ha, 2x5tn cr, 2x5tn der, 10,900bhp AESA-B&W, 18kn. (Tolerton)**

No claims would be advanced for the *Iberian Reefer* (above) and *Italian Reefer* of 1985 as being among the most attractive reefers. Built in Bilbao for Cadiz owner Extremena as the *Extresol* and *Extreluz* respectively, they were immediately chartered to Lauritzen with traditional JL names, the *Iberian Reefer* carrying fruit from Valparaiso to Savona, Italy, on her first voyage. In 1988 they went to Chargeurs Reunis as the *CR Alicante* and *CR Dieppe*, and in 1991 to Delmas-Vieljeux before a further sale to the Restis group's Enterprises Shipping & Trading in 1993 as the *Brest* and *Bretagne*.

Hansa Bremen -- **Schiffahrtsgesellschaft 'Hamme" GmbH & Co KG (Leonhardt & Blumberg), Liberia; Bremer Vulkan, Bremen, 1989; 10,842gt, 12,942 dwt, 156m, 4ha, 2x18tn cr, 9449bhp B&W, 21kn. (Kevin Moore)**

Modern German kuhlschiff construction has included the *Hansa Bremen* of 1989 and *Hansa Visby* (1989), *Hansa Lubeck* (1990), and *Hansa Stockholm* (1991), a quartet of 10,800gt, 21kn ships from Bremer Vulkan for Leonhardt & Blumberg KG companies. They can carry 290 containers. Some similar ships were completed by Schichau.

Walter Jacob -- **Partenreederei ms 'Walter Jacob' (Ernst Jacob), Germany; Flender Werft, Lubeck, 1984; 9417gt, 11,755dwt, 146m, 4ha, 3x10tn cr, 1x10 & 1x5tn der, 13,000bhp Mitsui-B&W, 21kn. (Tolerton)**

The *Walter Jacob* (above) of 1984 and *Helene Jacob* (below) of 1983 from Flender Werft have had interesting histories, being launched with the above names but completed for Ernst Jacob of Flensburg with the Scipio charter names *Bremerhaven* and *Blumenthal* respectively, and reverting to their Jacob names in 1988. From the mid-90s they operated for Star Reefers as the *Trojan Star* and *Tudor Star*, the *Helene Jacob* having had an earlier spell as a Blue Star trader as the *Saxon Star*. The pair have side doors port and starboard for each hold, fuel consumption of 41tn a day, and were among the earliest recipients of a "kamikaze" lifeboat.

Helene Jacob -- **Partenreederei ms 'Blumenthal' (Ernst Jacob), Germany; Flender Werft, Lubeck, 1983; 9417gt, 11,805dwt, 145m, 4ha, 3x10tn cr, 1x10 & 1x5tn der, 13,000bhp Mitsui-B&W, 21kn. (Tolerton)**

Soviet reefer contrasts -- the *Larisa Reysner* of 1970 (foreground), one of a class of 12 flush-decked, Polish-built ships, and the more elegant *Parkhomenko* of 1968, one of a class of five Soviet reefers built in Italy. (Tolerton)

CHAPTER FOUR

SOVIET AND EAST EUROPEAN REEFERS

The Soviet Union built up the largest fleet of refrigerated ships in the world, the majority of them utilitarian fish carriers built in the 1960s, 70s, and 80s to support its world-ranging fishing fleet. By the end of the 1980s and shortly before the collapse of the Soviet Union, a quarter of the world's reefer ships flew the hammer and sickle flag. Like its factory trawlers, the fish carriers were built in series, with construction at Soviet shipyards -- primarily at the 61 Kommunar yard at the Black Sea port of Nikolayev, now part of the Ukraine -- augmented by construction in East Germany and Poland, with Sweden and France also contributing. In the 60s and 70s a number of conventional West German and Norwegian reefers were also purchased for service as fish carriers. By the late 1980s, the USSR's fish carrier fleet numbered more than 200 ships.

Aside from the dedicated fish carriers, the Soviet Union also commissioned several significant classes of conventional reefer ships in the 1960s, 70s, and 80s, primarily from Poland but also from Italian, Danish, and Greek shipbuilders. The employment of these state-owned vessels in cross-trades drew complaints of unfair competition from West European operators who faced considerably higher manning costs.

Arkhip Kuindzhi -- **Dalryba, USSR; 61 Kommunar, Nikolayev, 1965; 6160gt, 5170dwt, 130m, 4ha, 8x3tn & 1x1tn der, 7200bhp 4 x Fairbanks, 16.5kn. (Tolerton)**

The typical Soviet fish carrier -- the Vladivostok-registered *Arkhip Kuindzhi* of 1965 was one of the ships of the numerically largest class, a series of 38 diesel-electric, ice-strengthened 6000gt ships built at the 61 Kommunar yard, Nikolayev, over a 10 year span from 1963. Nine or so others were built for Bulgaria, East Germany, and Romania. Four 10 cylinder motors drove four generators each connected to two electric motors and geared to the screw shaft.

Sibir -- **Dalryba, USSR; 61 Kommunar, Nikolayev, 1963; 6133gt, 5285dwt, 130m, 4ha, 8x3 & 1x1tn der, 7200bhp 4 engines, 16.5kn. (Tolerton)**

The lead ship of the diesel-electric 6000gt class shown on the previous page was the *Sibir* of 1963, pictured (top) working fishing vessels at a New Zealand port in the 1980s.

Among the earliest purpose-built Soviet fish carriers were a class of six 3700gt ships built in West Germany in the 1950s (probably as war reparations) by Orenstein-Koppel. The first was the *Jana* (centre) of 1955.

The *Komsomolskaya Smena* of 1984 (below) was the last of a class of five small 2300gt fish carriers from the Zelenodolskiy shipyard that began with the *Tatarstan* of 1977. The large accommodation block suggests the ships of this class also acted as ferries for crew changes in the fishing fleets.

Jana -- **Dalryba, USSR; Orenstein-Koppel, Lubeck, 1955; 3782gt, 3616dwt, 111m, 5ha (3ho), 1x25 & 10x3tn der, 3120bhp MAN, 14kn. (Tolerton)**

Komsomolskaya Smena -- **Vostokrybkholodflot, USSR; Zelenodolskiy, Zelenodolsk, 1984; 2379gt, 1880dwt, 95m, 3ha, 6x5tn der, 3000bhp Skoda, 13.5kn. (Tolerton)**

Proliv Longa -- **Cape Ocean Maritime, Panama; 61 Kommunar, Nikolayev, 1983; 13,496gt, 11,560dwt, 172m, 4ha, 8x5tn der, 10,600bhp Bryansk-B&W, 18.75kn. (Tolerton)**

Representatives of two later fish carrier designs from 61 Kommunar: The *Proliv Longa* of 1983 (above) was one of the last completions in a series of 19 much larger and faster 13,000gt vessels -- products of the neo-Stalinist school of naval architecture, it has to be said -- from the Nikolayev yard starting with the *50 Let SSSR* of 1974. She is pictured in the Ukrainian state fisheries funnel livery in the 1990s. The *Anton Gurin* of 1988 (below) was one of a series of about 25 smaller vessels completed by the yard from 1985, many for Laskaridis.

Anton Gurin -- **Vostokrybkholodflot, Panama; 61 Kommunar, Nikolayev, 1988; 6670gt, 4900dwt, 126m, 4ha, 8x2tn der, 5384bhp Bryansk-B&W, 15kn. (Kees Lous)**

Kolskiy Zaliv -- **Ponoy Shipping Co (Mayflower Shipmanagement), Cyprus; Mathias-Thesen, Wismar, 1986; 12,410gt, 9360dwt, 152m, 4ha, 2x10 & 7x5tn der, 10,332bhp DMR-MAN, 17.7kn. (Tolerton)**

The largest class of East German-built fish carriers for the Soviet Union consisted of the 35 or so Kristal class ships from VEB Mathias-Thesen, like the *Kolskiy Zaliv* of 1986 (above) and the *Atmoda*, originally the *Rizhskiy Bereg*, of 1989 (below) pictured in the Laskaridis-owned Riga Transport Fleet funnel colours. The series started with the *Almaznyy Bereg* of 1978. Another 20-odd ships to the similar Polar design, different notably for some streamlining of the superstructure, were also completed by Mathias-Thesen in 1970-77. The first ship was the *Karl Liebknecht* of 1970. Note the extensive accommodation.

Atmoda -- **Riga Transport Fleet , Panama; Mathias-Thesen, Wismar, 1989; 12,413gt, 9202dwt, 152m, 4ha, 2x10 & 7x5tn der, 10,332bhp DMR-MAN, 17.4kn. (Tolerton)**

Professor Popov -- **Far Eastern Shipping Co, USSR; Stocznia Gdanska, Gdansk, 1977; 6400gt, 5880dwt, 139m, 4ha (2ho), 8x5tn der, 13,200bhp Cegielski-Sulzer, 20.75kn. (Tolerton)**

Poland built two important series of reefers in the 1970s primarily for the Soviet Union, the 6400gt B437 types like the *Professor Popov* (above) and the flush-decked 5200gt B443 series for which the *Aleksandra Kollontay* (below) of 1970 was the lead ship. The B437s started with the *Nikolay Kopernik* of 1974 and numbered 14 ships for the USSR, three for Poland, and three for Empresa Hondurena. The B443 series ran to 12 ships, all for the USSR.

Aleksandra Kollontay -- **Latvian Shipping Co, USSR; Stocznia Gdanska, Gdansk, 1970; 2984/5215gt, 4151dwt, 119m, 4ha, 8x5tn der, 8400bhp B&W, 19kn. (Tolerton)**

Yanis Lentsmanis -- **Far-Eastern Shipping Co, Russia; Stocznia Gdanska, Gdansk, 1971; 2948/5194gt 4413dwt, 119m, 4ha, 8x5tn der, 8400bhp B&W, 19kn. (Tolerton)**

Two of the B443 types later in their careers under the Russian flag after the Soviet collapse -- and both looking rather careworn. A new coat of white paint on the hull hardly disguises the wrinkles of the *Yanis Lentsmanis* of 1971 (above), now with the post-Soviet Fesco funnel. Renamed *Polluks* in 1998, she was scrapped after being seriously damaged by fire in the Okhotsk Sea in 2003. The *Otomar Oshkaln* of 1973 (below) is also pictured Fesco-owned.

Otomar Oshkaln -- **Far-Eastern Shipping Co, Russia; Stocznia Gdanska, Gdansk, 1973; 2948/5194gt, 4251dwt, 119m, 4ha, 8x3tn der, 8400bhp B&W, 19kn. (Tolerton)**

Zyrardow -- **Polish Ocean Lines, Poland; Arsenal do Alfeite, Lamada, 1980; 3299/6414gt, 5640dwt, 139m, 4ha, 8x3tn der, 13,200bhp Cegielski-Sulzer, 22.5kn. (Tolerton)**

A curiosity among the B437 types and nearly the last ship listed in every register was the *Zyrardow* of 1980 of Polish Ocean Lines, which with one sister was contracted out to a Spanish yard, while a third for POL was built in Portugal. She had four sidedoors each side. Showing POL's handsome gold, red, and white funnel to advantage above a very weathered hull in this photograph, she was lost in 2001 as the *Ocean Breeze* after running aground near Zuqar Island, Yemen.

Kurpie -- **Transocean Fruits Co (Deep Sea Services & Fish Handling Co, Szczecin), Cyprus; Stocznia Gdanska, Gdansk, 1988; 8864gt, 6333dwt, 139m, 4ha, 9900bhp Cegielski-B&W, 18kn. (Tolerton)**

In the 1980s Stocznia Gdanska built six fish carriers in its B364 series, including the *Kurpie* of 1988, seen in the colours of Japan's Kyokuyo group, and like many other former Soviet block ships flagged out to Cyprus.

Polar Chile -- **Polar Chile Shipping Inc (Columbus Ship Mgmt), Liberia; Stocznia Gdanska, Gdansk, 1993; 10,629gt, 10,582dwt, 150m, 4ha, 4x8tn cr, 15,498bhp Cegielski-Sulzer, 21.8kn. (Kevin Moore)**

Prominent among the modern reefer ship completions in Poland have been vessels of the B369 type like the *Polar Chile* of 1993 (above) and the *Dole Africa* of 1994 (below). The *Polar Chile* was one of six built for Norway's Reksten with its traditional Emperor names (in her case *Trajan*) and later operating for Hamburg-Sud. She was designed to carry 178 TEUs and fuel consumption was 51tn a day. The *Dole Africa* and her sisters *Dole America*, *Dole Asia*, and *Dole Europa* were improved versions designed to carry up to 264 containers.

Dole Africa -- **Dole Fresh Fruit Int, Bahamas; Stocznia Gdanksa, Gdansk, 1994; 10,584gt, 10,282dwt, 150m, 4ha, 2x32, 2x8tn cr, 15,515bhp Hyundai-B&W, 21.8kn. (Kees Lous)**

Horncap -- **Pluto Shipping Corp (Horn-Linie), Liberia; Brodogradiliste Uljanik, Pula, 1991; 12,887gt, 9160dwt, 154m, 7ha (4ho) & stern ramp, 4x25tn cr, 12,064bhp B&W, 20kn. (Kees Lous)**

Notable among other East European reefer completions of the 1990s were an unusual trio for Germany's Horn Line from Croatian shipbuilder Brodogradiliste Uljanik, designed for Caribbean-UK/Europe service. The *Hornbay* of 1990, *Horncap* (above) of 1991, and *Horncliff* of 1992 are 12,887gt reefers with a starboard quarter stern ramp for ro-ro cargo, provision for 322 containers and nearly 300 vehicles, and four twinned 25tn cranes. The four holds were fully insulated for reefer cargo, while vehicles are carried on decks around the engine casings, and doors in the forward engineroom bulkhead also gave access to the cargo hold decks for vehicles. The ships could also carry 12 passengers. Fuel consumption was 46tn a day.

An earlier completion from Brodogradiliste's Split yard was the *Mahone Bay* (below) of 1981, originally Mediteranska Plovidba's *Racisce*, and to the same design as Boelwerf's *Pocantico* class.

Mahone Bay -- **ms 'Mahone Bay' NTH Schiffahrts GmbH & Co KG (Thien & Heyenga), Antigua & Barbuda; Brodogradiliste Split, Split, 1981; 10,651gt, 9835dwt, 151m, 4ha, 4x5tn cr, 16,533bhp MAN, 20kn. (Kees Lous)**

Atlanta -- **Polar Star SA, Bahamas; Murakami Hide Zosen, Hakata, 1991; 3948gt, 5411dwt, 103m, 3ha, 6x5tn der, 4900bhp Akasaka-Mitsubishi, 15kn. (Tolerton)**

Typical of the small Japanese-built reefers that dominate the world fleet today is the 3948gt *Atlanta*, arriving at a New Zealand port in 1991 to load squash at the end of her voyage from the shipbuilder's yard.

CHAPTER FIVE

JAPANESE-BUILT REEFERS

As in other spheres of shipbuilding, Japan came to dominate reefer construction, and today the work horse of the world's conventional reefer fleet is the Japanese reefer. Size typically ranges from 3000gt to less than 9000gt, but the overall appearance of these three or four hatch engines-aft ships with their array of derricks is characteristic, and like the Liberty ships, they sometimes appear to have been built by the mile and chopped off by the yard. However, there is more variety of builder and design among these vessels than outward appearance would suggest. They may not be as glamorous as the yacht-like reefer ships of the past, but now they dominate the world fleet, and while container ships have swept up more and more of the reefer trades, these vessels have been very successful in the niches left for conventional reefers.

Construction of small engines-aft reefers developed in the 1960s for domestic owners, and foreign orders like P&O/New Zealand Shipping Co's for the *Manapouri* and *Mataura* saw much larger reefers on the stocks at Japanese yards before the end of this decade. Construction of the larger engines-aft Japanese-built reefers that have now become ubiquitous in the world reefer trades really developed in the 80s, when their success with charterers like Lauritzen popularised ships of this type with the big reefer operators.

As with other types of ship built in Japan, reefers tend to be the specialty of particular yards. Midsize and smaller builders, notably Hayashikane, Kochi, Kyokuyo, Shikoku, Kitanihon, and Shin Kurushima have been to the fore in reefer construction.

Many of the Japanese reefers have been built as fish carriers to support the fishing fleets of Japan and other countries which range the oceans of the world for whitefish, tuna, and squid. As well as saving high seas fishing vessels frequent trips to port to discharge their catches by transshipping it at sea instead, the fish carriers also serve as supply vessels for the fleet. They can refuel them, bring out fresh crews, and provide stores, water, new equipment and parts, and bait.

The typical fish carrier is an engines-aft ship of under 5000dwt with three hatches served by 5tn derricks, and can freeze the catch down to minus 40deg C in its holds. They have their call signs prominently painted on the superstructure for aerial identification in territorial waters, and conspicuous are the large Yokohama fenders on deck which are lowered over the side to keep them and the fishing boats apart during transshipment operations.

Fish carriers operate under a variety of flags, but are generally in the funnel colours of one of the Japanese fishing giants like Kyokuyo, Nissui, Maruha/Taiyo, and Nichiro which charter them.

***Itohamu Maru No.1* -- Sonoda Kisen KK, Japan; Miho Zosensho, Shimizu, 1968; 2592gt, 3344dwt, 100m, 3ha, 3x2tn cr, 3800bhp Kobe Hatsudoki, 14.75kn. (Tolerton)**

Two early examples of Japanese-built reefers. The *Itohamu Maru No.1* (above) and the *Juyo Maru* (below) were both 1968 completions, but while the former from Miho has the characteristic engines-aft appearance of the hundreds of small reefers and fish carriers that have followed her from Japanese yards, the *Juyo Maru* from Hayashikane was a raised quarter-deck vessel with two holds forward and one aft. The *Itohamu Maru No.1* had three small cranes, but derricks are much more usual for cargo-handling on the smaller Japanese reefers. The green hull and black funnel with white emblem of the *Juyo Maru* show she was operating for Japanese fisheries giant Taiyo.

***Juyo Maru* -- Mitsubishi Shintaku Ginko KK, Japan; Hayashikane SB, Shimonoseki, 1968; 3411gt, 4512dwt, 111m, 3ha, 6x3tn der, 6000bhp Kobe Hatsudoki, 16kn. (Tolerton)**

Win Master -- **Win Master Reefer Line (Win Far Fishery Group), Panama; Taihei Kogyo, Akitsu, 1973; 2987gt, 4220dwt, 109m, 3ha, 6x3tn der, 5800bhp Kobe Hatsudoki, 16kn. (Tolerton)**

The 2900gt *Soyokaze* of 1972 and *Win Master* of 1973 are fundamentally similar in appearance to the reefers/fish carriers of their size built over the following decades in Japan. Both had very long lives, and when photographed in 2005 (above) the *Win Master*, built as the *Hayatsuki Maru*, was sailing under her fifth name and operating for Taiwan's Win Far Fishery Group of Kaohsiung. Conspicuous on the deck of the plainly hard-worked *Soyokaze* (below), renamed from *Soyokaze Maru* in 1989, are the large rubber Yokohama fenders essential during cargo transshipment from fishing vessels. In the 90s the *Soyokaze* operated for South Korea's O Yang Fisheries.

Soyokaze -- **Soyokaze Marine Corp (NS Marine), Liberia; Taguma Zosen, Innoshima, 1972; 2907gt, 4248dwt, 97m, 3ha, 6x5tn der, 5600bhp Niigata, 14.75kn. (Tolerton)**

Oceano Artico -- **Empresa Flota Cubana de Pesca, Cuba; Kanda Zosensho, Kure, 1977; 10,549gt, 10,540dwt, 163m, 4ha, 4x5tn der, 15,500bhp Hitachi-B&W, 23.25kn. (Tolerton)**

Japanese yards were soon building considerably larger ships than the previous vessels. A significant and interesting class was a group of seven fast 10,000gt ships, five from Kanda for the Cuban state fleet including the *Oceano Artico* (above) of 1977, and two from Onomichi, the Japanese-owned, Panamanian-flag *Pacific Reefer* (below) and *Sonoda Reefer* of 1974. They had four holds, three forward and one aft of the engineroom, and four sidedoors each side, and were followed by a large number of similarly configured but slightly smaller reefers for charter from other Japanese yards in the next few years.

Pacific Reefer -- **Triumph Naviera SA (Chiyoda Senpaku Co), Panama; Onomichi Zosen, Onomichi, 1974; 10,053gt, 10,736dwt, 162m, 4ha, 4x5tn der, 15,500bhp Hitachi-B&W, 20.5kn. (Tolerton)**

Tokyo Reefer -- **Shinsei Kaiun Co, Japan; Naikai SB, Setoda, 1978; 7191gt, 8078dwt, 144m, 4ha, 8x5tn der, 10,700bhp Hitachi-B&W, 19kn. (Tolerton)**

Demand for new reefer tonnage saw a rash of more than 150 ships delivered in the reefer madness (that line had to be slipped in somewhere in this book!) of 1978-1980, and the 1979 world output of 465,000dwt of new reefer tonnage was the highest ever. Japanese yards made a significant contribution with vessels like the 7191gt *Tokyo Reefer* of 1978 (above) from Naikai, one of five sisters, the others being built by Hitachi. This class, too, had sidedoors port and starboard for each of the four holds. The *Ikoma Maru* of 1979 (below) from Hitachi and her sister *Asama Maru* (1978) from Naikai (an associate of Hitachi) were slightly larger and more powerful versions of the previous five, with a longer forecastle. The *Ikoma Maru* has the red and white funnel of Lauritzen-Peninsular Reefers, the white triangles being a stylized LPR.

Ikoma Maru -- **Nippon Suisan KK, Japan; Hitachi Zosen, Maizuru, 1979; 8369gt, 9282dwt, 150m, 4ha, 12x9tn der, 15,000bhp IHI Pielstick, 20kn. (Tolerton)**

African Princess -- **Princess Line, Liberia; Kochi Jyuko, Kochi, 1979; 9018gt, 9125dwt, 151m, 4ha, 4x10tn cr, 18,000bhp IHI-Pielstick, 20kn. (Tolerton)**

Other Japanese reefers of this generation included the *African Princess* (above) of 1979, one of a class of three built by Kochi Jyuko as the *Hawaii*, *Barrios*, and *Turbo*. Twenty knot ships consuming 55tns of fuel a day, they, too, had eight sidedoors for the four holds, but cranes instead of derricks. The *Hawaii* became the *African Princess* in 1989. Similar but smaller was the *Frio Ipanema* (below) of 1978 from Kurushima, built as the *Puma* with a sister, *Panther*, for Kitanihon-Oi Kaiun. She went to Alang in 2003 as the *Ocean Ice*.

Frio Ipanema -- **Rossoyne Maritime, Bahamas; Kurushima Dock, Uwajima, 1978; 7194gt, 7764dwt, 143m, 4ha, 4x5tn cr, 11,700bhp IHI-Pielstick, 20kn. (Tolerton)**

Bora Universal -- **Kildare Ltd, Bermuda; Mitsubishi HI, Hiroshima, 1979; 8429gt, 9175wt, 154m, 4ha, 2x5tn cr & 8x5tn der, 15,200bhp Mitsubishi-Sulzer, 21kn. (author's collection)**

The *Bora Universal* of 1979 and her sister *Scirocco Universal* completed the same year stood out in contrast to their functional contemporaries from the Japanese yards. Both from Mitsubishi for Safmarine/Union-Castle's Universal Reefers, they were more traditional in appearance and perhaps the last reefers from Japanese yards with some concession made to elegance.

Walili -- **Cie de Transport Maritime SA (Soc Marocaine de Navigation Maritime), Morocco; Miho Zosensho, Shimizu, 1980; 2075gt, 3020dwt, 91m, 2ha, 3840bhp Hanshin, 15.25kn. (Kees Lous)**

Disproportionately tall kingposts distinguished the Tangier-registered *Walili*, a small 1980 reefer and one of two similar completions from Miho for Moroccan operator Navimar.

Nippon Reefer -- **Sanwa Senpaku KK, Japan; Kyokuyo Zosen, Chofu, 1982; 8012gt, 8657dwt, 142m, 4ha, 8x5tn der, 8100bhp IHI-Pielstick, 17.25kn. (Tolerton)**

The *Nippon Reefer* (above) and *New Zealand Reefer* were a pair of highly influential ships, establishing the credentials of relatively large engine-aft vessels with European reefer operators. The sisters from Kyokuyo were delivered in 1982 to Lauritzen on long-term charter and later purchased, the first of many engine-aft ships like this for JL. They had four port side sidedoors. On her maiden voyage the *Nippon Reefer* carried apples from Seattle and bananas from Golfito to Scandinavia. A slightly larger tramp reefer which also saw service for European operators was the *Cap Frio*, which revived a famous Hamburg-Sud name. She was launched as the *Ocean Bride* and completed in 1983 by Shin Yamamoto as the *Ocean Pride*, becoming the *Oceanic Trader* in 1992 before getting her Hamburg-Sud name a year later. Her sisters *Nordenham* and *Nienburg* began their careers chartered to German owners.

Cap Frio -- **Arrow Navigation SA (Target Marine), Bahamas; Shin Yamamoto, Kochi, 1983; 9755gt, 12,181dwt, 149m, 4ha, 8x5tn der, 11,300bhp Hitachi-B&W, 18kn. (Tolerton)**

Cap Triunfo -- Lepta Shipping Co (Orient Marine Co), Panama; Shin Kurushima Dockyard, Onishi, 1988; 8487gt, 9734dwt, 141m, 4ha, 10,800bhp Hatsudoki-Mitsubishi, 19kn. (Tolerton)

Two classes of larger Japanese reefers from later in the 80s are represented by the *Cap Triunfo* (above) from Shin Kurushima and *Tasman Universal* (below) from Hayashikane, both 1988 completions. The *Cap Triunfo*, one of about 10 similar ships from Shin Kurushima and Sasebo, started charter voyaging for Hamburg-Sud on completion, but, illustrating the vagaries of shipping, was sporting a Great White Fleet funnel, "Horn Linie" on her hull, and still a Hamburg-Sud name when photographed a few years later. Distinctive for their ugly oversize funnels, the *Tasman Universal* (below) and sisters *Arctic Universal*, *Baltic Universal*, and *Lincoln Universal* were built for Universal Reefers, and sold in 1997 to Unicoolship, with the Universal suffixes changing to Spirit. The *Tasman Universal* could carry 66 TEUs on deck and the *Cap Triunfo* 36.

Tasman Universal -- Kulan Corporation (Gateway Shipping), Sri Lanka; Hayashikane SB, Shimonoseki, 1988; 9622gt, 11,055dwt, 145m, 4ha, 2x30tn, 2x10tn cr, 10,670bhp Mitsui-B&W, 18.5kn. (Kevin Moore collection)

***Thorgull* -- Tonnevold Reefer 4 KS (O T Tonnevold AS), Liberia; Shikoku Dockyard, Takamatsu, 1983; 6127gt, 6325dwt, 145m, 4ha, 8x5tn der, 7890bhp Mitsui-B&W, 17.5kn. (Tolerton)**

While Western European shipping companies have tended to take Japanese reefers on charter rather than owning them, Norwegian owner O T Tonnevold of Grimstad has diligently acquired them secondhand, including the 1983-built *Thorgull* (above), bought in 1996, and the 1993-built *Thorbjorg* (below), added in 2005. The *Thorgull*, which previously operated on charter to Lauritzen as the *Reefer Penguin*, is one of a group of six exceptionally fine-lined reefers from Shikoku, and like many of Tonnevold's ships operated on charter to Nissui. The *Thorbjorg*, previously the *Pentland Phoenix*, is one of a large class of about 20 very similar ships from Shin Kochi, Shin Kurushima, Kitanihon, and Kanasashi with a long forecastle, conspicuous trunked hatches, and fuel consumption of about 25tn a day.

***Thorbjorg* -- Tonnevold Reefer 6 KS (OT Tonnevold), Panama; Shin Kochi Jyuko, Kochi, 1993; 7313gt, 8045dwt, 134m, 4ha, 8x5tn der, 9599bhp Mitsubishi, 19kn. (Tolerton)**

Auckland -- **Mi-Das Line, Panama; Kanasashi, Shimizu, 1993; 7307gt, 5388dwt, 134m, 4ha, 8x5tn der, 8156bhp Akasaka-Mitsubishi, 18kn. (Tolerton)**

A different angle on another ship of this class, the Japanese-owned, Panama-flagged *Auckland* (above), in the colours of Nissui-Seatrade joint venture Federated Fruitcarriers. Kyokuyo Zosen's contribution in this size range has been ships like the *Chikuma Reefer* of 1998 (below), rather stylish for a modern vessel. She is operating for Kyokuyo Shipping with its distinctive stylised dragonfly funnel emblem. Established just before the war for whaling, Kyokuyo entered ocean fishing in 1954 and reefer transport in 1973, and the company is one of Japan's giants in the seafood industry.

Chikuma Reefer -- **MH Maritima SA (Honma Senpaku), Panama; Kyokuyo Zosen, Chofu, 1998; 7367gt, 8097dwt, 135m, 4ha, 8x5tn der, 9599bhp Akasaka-Mitsubishi, 19kn. (Tolerton)**

Punente -- **Rising Sun Line SA (Shinsei Kaiun), Panama; Towa Zosen, Shimonoseki, 1984; 7736gt, 8556dwt, 139m, 4ha, 8x7tn der, 8500bhp Hatsudoki-Mitsubishi, 17kn. (Tolerton)**

Towa Zosen contributed the 17kn, 7700gt trio of *Levante* (1983), *Punente*, and *Juvante* (both 1984) -- the latter renamed *Chiricana* in 1987 -- for Japanese ownership. They were also set up for vehicle carrying like many Japanese reefers and could take 53 containers. The distinctive funnel colours of Nissui Shipping are prominent in this view of the *Punente*.

Amber Atlantic -- **Amber Ocean Corp (Phoenix Co), Panama; Shin Kurushima Dockyard, Akitsu, 1989; 5476gt, 6756dwt, 124m, 4ha, 7000bhp Hatsudoki-Mitsubishi, 16.9kn. (Tolerton)**

Picking up speed down a choppy New Zealand harbour is the *Amber Atlantic*, another reefer of this era also designed to carry vehicles as well as refrigerated cargoes, thus reducing ballast passages.

Saltlake -- Whitebay Shipping SA, Panama; Kochi Jyuko, Kochi, 1986; 3511gt, 4269dwt, 96m, 3ha, 6x5tn der, 4050bhp Akasaka-Mitsubishi, 14.75kn. (Tolerton)

Three typical fish carriers, all in Taiyo colours, the *Saltlake* (top) built in 1986 as the *Katah* and renamed in 1990, *Reefer Queen* (centre), and *Kyokushin* (bottom), which was completed in 1979 as the *Kyokushin Maru* and dropped the suffix in 1992. All are Panamanian-flagged, three hatch vessels with six 5tn derricks.

Reefer Queen -- Seto Marine SA, Panama; Kyokuyo Zosen, Chofu, 1991; 4446gt, 5248dwt, 120m, 3ha, 6x5tn der, 5603bhp Mitsubishi, 15.8kn. (Tolerton)

Kyokushin -- Atlas Shipping Maritime SA, Panama; Kochi Jyuko, Kochi, 1979; 3437gt, 3853dwt, 99m, 3ha, 6x5tn der, 4500bhp Mitsubishi, 14.9kn. (Tolerton)

81

Emanuel B and *Arctic C* **(Tolerton)**

Differences between earlier and slightly larger later versions of the Drammen design are apparent in this 1989 photo of the *Arctic C*, completed in 1971 as the *Nordland*, and the *Emanuel B*, built in 1976 as the *Emanuel*, sharing a wharf. The latter has 5tn cranes instead of derricks, different ventilators, and a rectangular funnel with lattice top. Both have five sidedoors port and starboard.

CHAPTER SIX
THE DRAMMEN REEFERS

The biggest success story in the history of reefer design has been the Drammen reefers. Forty ships were completed over 12 years from 1968 to this design from Drammen Slip & Verksted of Drammen, near Oslo -- most at the Drammen yard but some at other Norwegian yards and a series of eight at Smith's Dock, Middlesbrough.

The fast Drammens were familiar for more than 30 years in ports worldwide, uplifting every sort of refrigerated cargo, and although eventually superseded by larger, more versatile ships better fitted for pallets and containers, they were part of the backbone of the world pure reefer fleet for a long time. Popular with charterers, they served under flags as diverse as those of Britain, Norway, West and East Germany, the USSR, Portugal, Israel, Greece, Singapore, Yugoslavia, Ecuador, Iraq, and Morocco, as well as the flags of convenience like Panama, Liberia, Cyprus, and the Bahamas. Their sleek lines and conspicuous chine aft to maximise capacity in the aft hold made them readily identifiable ships, in spite of some variations as the series evolved. They were notoriously tender ships.

Standard ship construction had been applied to reefer building before, notably with the American-built R1 and R2 designs of World War Two, but the success of the Drammen design in peacetime is unique. The first completions, both for Norwegian owner Gotaas-Larsen, were the *Golar Nel* in February 1968 from Drammen and the *Golar Freeze* later the same year from Marinens Hovedverft, Horten (its only completion to the design). This first pair differed from later vessels in being flushdecked, whereas the rest of the series, like many subsequent reefer designs, had a long forecastle extending aft of No.1 hatch.

Gotaas-Larsen and Israeli operator Maritime Fruit Carriers monopolized the Drammen output for the first five years, but the 15th and 16th completions brought the design new attention when they were delivered as the *Wild Flamingo* and *Wild Fulmar* in 1973 and 1974 for Federal Steam Navigation Co in P&O's General Cargo Division. Unlike Federal's great refrigerated steamers and motorships that had run between Britain and Australia-New Zealand for a century, the two newcomers were intended for worldwide tramping at a time of enormous change for traditional shipping companies. They entered service with the Federal funnel, but were to be more familiar in the new P&O yellow hull and blue funnel with white P&O logo.

The particulars of the *Wild Flamingo*, typical of the Drammens, were: Gross tonnage, open and closed shelter deck, 5014 and 6925gt; overall length, 144m (with bulbous bow); breadth, 18m; draught, 8.25m/9m; engine, 13,200bhp 8cy Sulzer; speed, 23kn.

Four holds served by eight 5tn derricks and eight winches gave 10,802 cu/m of cargo space. There were also five side doors port and starboard, No.1 hold being served by two.

The success of this pair led P&O to order two more Drammens, and the *Wild Gannet* of 1976 and *Wild Grebe* of 1978 were of an improved version of the design. The conspicuous improvement on the earlier two was the fitting of four 5tn cranes instead of derricks, and the profile was enhanced by a streamlined trim on the top of the funnel. Cosmetic attention to the funnel was a feature of the later improved Drammens -- most, if not all, of the rest had a lattice top to the funnel.

The Drammen yard was owned by Peter Berg, who took delivery of some of the later completions -- *Emanuel* (1976), *Ragni Berg* (1978), *Elisabeth Berg* (1979) -- for his own companies.

It speaks for the success of the Drammens that the first pair, *Golar Nel* and *Golar Freeze*, both served for 25 years before going to the breakers in 1993. Most of their successors had similarly long careers.

From Marinens Hovedverft, Horten:
164 - 1968 *Golar Freeze*, *Limon* 1976, to Alang for b/u 93.

From Drammen Slip & Verksted, Drammen:
63 - 1968 *Golar Nel*, *Brestskaya Krepost* 75, *S.Lucia* 90, to Aliaga for b/u 93.

64 - 1968 *Golar Frost*, *Bolivar* 76, *Rio Daule* 85, to Alang for b/u 98.

65 - 1969 *Alaskacore* (launched as *Slevik*), *Alaska* 75, *Alaska* 1 79, *Alaska* 84, *Nissos Skopelos* 86, sank NE of Azores, voyage Amsterdam-Cuba 86.

66 - 1969 *Golar Borg*, abandoned west of Azores, voyage Rostock-Havana 78.

67 - 1970 *Antarcticore*, *Antarctic* 75, *Nissos Skiathos* 86, *Skiathos Reefer* 88, in collision & sank Nantong River, Shanghai, after sale for b/u 93.

68 - 1970 *Beringcore*, *Bering* 75, *Bonita* 75, sank English Channel, voyage Hamburg-Costa Rica 81.

69 - 1971 *Greenland*, *Cayman* 75, *Smara* 76, *Ithaka Reefer* 87, *Pacific Trader* 91, to Alang for b/u 94.

70 - 1971 *Iceland*, *Atitlan* 84, *Iceland* 85, *Urucitrus* 85, *Nissos Naxos* 88, *Naxos Reefer* 88, *Atlantic Trader* 91, to Ningbo for b/u 93.

71 - 1971 *Nordland*, *Nordland V* 79, *Arawak* 84, *Nordland V* 85, *Nissos Paros* 87, *Arctic C* 89, *Arctic Reefer* 90, sank off Kyushu voyage China-Venezuela 94.

72 - 1972 *Lapland*, *Kungshamn* 76, *Sijilmassa* 78, *Bolivar Trader* 90, *Farid F* 94, *Torrens* 06.

73 - 1972 *Labrador Clipper*, *Tuscan Star* 76, *Chios Pride* 80, to Mumbai for b/u 93.

74 - 1972 *Golar Ragni* (launched as *Kongsfjell*), *Ragni Berg* 76, *Sierra Nevada* 77, *Puerto Cabello* (Venezuelan navy) 86.

75 - 1973 *Golar Girl*, *Hilco Girl* 77, *Timur Girl* 81, *Lucky* 83, *Lucky I* 84, *Ciudad de Guayaquil* 84, *Provincia del Guayas* 88, *Baltic Sea* 95.

76 - 1973 *Wild Flamingo*, *Reefer Ciku* 83, *Frio Chile* 87, *Las Palmas* 93, *Frio Chile* 94, sank NW Pacific, voyage Callao-Hachinohe 95.

77 - 1974 *Wild Fulmar*, *Reefer Duku* 83, *Starsea* 88, abandoned after fire voyage Corinto-Zeebrugge 90, to Alang for b/u 92 as Midway.

78 - 1974 *Frigoartico*, *Cap Frio* 82, *Tropical Sintra* 85, to Alang for b/u 99.

79 - 1974 *Frigoantartico*, *Cap Ferrato* 84, *Tropical Estoril* 85, to Alang for b/u 01.

81 - 1975 *Ifni*, *Brasilia Reefer* 90, to Mumbai for b/u 00.

82 - 1976 *Imilchil*, towed to Cristobal 90 after engineroom flooded, to Pakistan in tow 92 for scrapping but aground at Tema and offered for local sale 98.

83 - 1976 *Emanuel*, *Emanuel B* 85, *Emanuel C* 94, *UB Prince* 95, *Tbreed VII* 02.

84 - 1977 *Wild Gannet*, *Reefer Manggis* 83, *Ionic Reefer* 90, *Vergina Reefer* 97, to Aliaga for b/u 02 after laid up Eleusis 98.

85 - 1978 *Wild Grebe*, *Reefer Nangka* 83, *Aeolic Reefer* 90, *Minoic Reefer* 97, to India for b/u 03.

86 - 1977 *Imouzzer*, *Tropicana Reefer* 91, to Aliaga for b/u 02 after laid up Eleusis 98.

87 - 1978 *Ragni Berg*, *Bahamian Reefer* 87, *Otrant Frigo* 88, *Adriatic Trader* 93, *UB Polaris* 94, *Tbreed III* 02, to Alang for b/u 03.

90 - 1979 *Rio Esmeraldas*, *Isla Fernandina* 89, *Balboa Reefer* 95, *Kirki* 03, *Nordic Cape* 04.

91 - 1980 *Rio Chone*, *Isla Genovesa* 88, *Malibu Reefer* 95, *Malicia* 99, *Lilia 1* 99, *Ariadne* 02, *Nordic Star* 02.

92 - 1980 *Rio Babahoyo* (see Kaldnes completion)

93 - 1981 *Paquisha* (launched as *Rio Palora*), *Isla Isabela* 89, *Orenoco Reefer* 95, *Reno* 99, *Armonia* 02, *Nordic Ice* 02.

From Smith's Dock, Middlesbrough:

1318 - 1972 *Edinburgh Clipper*, *Alsatia* 77, *America Freezer* 81, *Angelmar* 85, *Atlantico* 90, *Network Swan* 90, *Banana Reefer* 92, to Chittagong for b/u 94.

1319 - 1972 *London Clipper*, *Salinas* 76, *Tropical Breeze* 78, *Rio Santa Rosa* 86, to Chittagong for b/u 93.

1320 - 1972 *Glasgow Clipper*, *Andania* 76, *Europa Freezer* 81, *Balmar* 85, *Pacifico* 90, *Network Stork* 90, *Banana Planter* 92, to Alang for b/u 95.

1321 - 1973 *Teesside Clipper*, *Andria* 77, *Australia Freezer* 81, *Chilly* 86, *Acechilly* 87, *Frio Hamburg* 88, *Bananor* 94, *UB Prudent* 98, *Pride III* 98, to Mumbai for b/u 99.

1322 - 1973 *Newcastle Clipper*, *Trojan Star* 76, *Chios Clipper* 80, *Frio Clipper* 92, *Roman Hurricane* 94, to Aliaga for b/u 95.

1323 - 1973 *Cardiff Clipper*, *Alaunia* 77, *Oceania Freezer* 81, *Frosty* 86, *Acefrosty* 87, *Frio Bremen* 88, *Golden B* 94, *UB Pearl* 98, to Alang for b/u 98.

1324 - 1973 *Bristol Clipper*, *King Edmund* 76, *Ernst Moritz Arndt* 77, *Bagno Catarama* 90, to Alang for b/u 94.

1325 - 1974 *Liverpool Clipper*, *King Egbert* 76, *Gerhart Hauptmann* 78, *Bagno Quevedo* 90, *Bille Frost* 92, hull damage from ice Cabot Strait, voyage Souris-Puerto Cabello, and to Alang for b/u 94.

From Framnaes, Sandefjord:

184 - 1975 *Heinrich Heine*, *Bagno El Triunfo* 90, *Metonic* 94, *Nafplio* 96.

185 - 1975 *Theodor Korner*, *Bagno Esmeraldas* 90, *Magellanic* 94, *Argolic* 96, *Vista 1* 99, *Eisha* 00.

From Kaldnes, Tonsberg:

214 - 1980 *Rio Babahoyo**, *Isla Pinta* 88, *Curacao Reefer* 95, *Kalypso* 03, *Nordic Bay* 04.

* This vessel was also given a Drammen yard number.

From Haugesund, Haugesund:

64 - 1979 *Elisabeth Berg*, *Zain Al-Qaws* 81, *Jawaher* 01, to India for b/u 03.

Ciudad de Guayaquil (ex-*Golar Girl*) of 1973. (Tolerton)

Limon -- **Dole Fresh Fruit International Ltd, Liberia; Marinens Hovedverft, Horten, 1968; 6709gt, 7244dwt, 139m, 4ha, 8x5tn der, 12,000bhp Sulzer, 21kn. (Tolerton)**

The first two Drammens, the *Golar Freeze* from Horten and the *Golar Nel* from Drammen, both completed in 1968, differed from the rest of the series in being flushdecked. Both were built for Norwegian owner Gotaas-Larsen and the former was sold in 1976 to become Dole's *Limon* (above), a name she retained until she went to the breakers in 1993.

Another early completion was the *Antarcticore* of 1970 for the ill-fated Maritime Fruit Carriers. Operating in the Lauritzen pool, she was on her fourth name as the Greek *Skiathos Reefer* (below).

Skiathos Reefer-- **Magna Compania Naviera SA (Transcontinental Maritime & Trading), Greece; Drammen, 1970; 4847gt, 7823dwt, 140m, 4ha, 8x5tn der, 12,000bhp Sulzer, 22.5kn. (Tolerton)**

Cayman - **Spanocean Line, UK; Drammen, 1971; 4876/6682gt, 9109dwt, 140m, 4ha, 8x5tn der, 14,850bhp Sulzer, 23kn. (World Ship Society)**

Provincia del Guayas -- **Naviera del Pacifico CA (Ecuadorian Line), Ecuador; Drammen, 1973; 4763/6599gt, 9218dwt, 140m, 4ha, 8x5tn der, 13,200bhp Horten-Sulzer, 22kn. (Tolerton)**

Many of the Drammen reefers had frequent changes of name during their careers. The *Greenland* of 1971 had five and is pictured (top) on her second as Spanocean's London-registered *Cayman*. The *Provincia del Guayas* (centre), built as the *Golar Girl* in 1973, was on her seventh and second in Noboa's Naviera del Pacifico fleet after being acquired by the Ecuadorians as *Ciudad de Guayaquil*. Completed in 1971 as the *Nordland*, the *Arctic C* (bottom) was on her sixth and, registered in Douglas, flew the British flag although apparently owned by Hungarian interests. All three have the typical Drammen features of eight 5tn derricks and five sidedoors port and starboard. Fuel consumption was 50tn a day.

Arctic C -- **Balance Reefer Services Ltd (Seascot Shiptrading), Isle of Man (UK); Drammen, 1971; 6676gt, 7701dwt, 140m, 4ha, 8x5tn der, 14,850bhp Sulzer, 22.5kn. (Tolerton)**

Wild Fulmar -- **Federal Steam Navigation Co (P&O General Cargo Division), UK; Drammen, 1974; 5014/6925gt, 9750dwt, 144m, 4ha, 8x5tn der, 13,200bhp Sulzer, 20kn. (Tolerton)**

Wild Flamingo -- **Federal Steam Navigation Co (P&O General Cargo Division), UK; Drammen, 1973; 5014/6925gt, 9750dwt, 144m, 4ha, 8x5tn der, 13,200bhp Sulzer, 23kn. (Tolerton)**

P&O took four of the Drammens in two pairs. The first were the *Wild Flamingo* of 1973 and the *Wild Fulmar* of 1974, both slightly longer versions of the basic design. They were followed by the *Wild Gannet* of 1977 and *Wild Grebe* of 1978, which had four 5tn cranes instead of the usual complement of eight 5tn derricks. The latter pair also had a fluted rim projecting aft of the funnel top as a difference. The *Wild Fulmar* is pictured top, and the *Wild Flamingo* centre, with the latter under later ownership as the *Frio Chile* at bottom. Under this name she was abandoned and sank in the north-west Pacific in 1995.

Frio Chile -- **Pineforest Shipping Co, Cyprus. (author's collection)**

Wild Grebe -- **Federal Steam Navigation Co (P&O General Cargo Division), UK; Drammen, 1978; 5017/6933gt, 9592dwt, 144m, 4ha, 4x5tn cr, 13,200bhp Sulzer, 22.75kn. (Tolerton)**

The second P&O pair were the *Wild Grebe* (above) and *Wild Gannet* (below). All four P&O Drammens were sold to in 1983 to Sembawang Reefer Lines of Singapore and renamed after tropical fruits, but they continued operating in the Lauritzen-Peninsular Reefers pool.

Wild Gannet -- **Midland Gillett Leasing (South) Ltd (P&O General Cargo Division), UK; Drammen, 1977; 5017/6933gt, 9592dwt, 144m, 4ha, 4x5tn cr, 13,200bhp Sulzer, 22.75kn. (Tolerton)**

Reefer Manggis -- **Sembawang Reefer Lines (Manggis) Pte Ltd (Sembawang Johnson Shipmanagement), Singapore. (Tolerton)**

Looking rather anorexic is the *Reefer Manggis* (above), the former *Wild Gannet*, after her sale to Sembawang. She went to the breakers at Aliaga in 2002, after being laid up since 1998.

One ship in the series was built by Haugesund, the *Elisabeth Berg* of 1979 for Peter Berg. She was sold two years later to an Iraqi state company as the *Zain Al-Qaws* (below), registered in Basrah. She traded for the Iraqis for 20 years and is pictured here operating in the Lauritzen-Peninsular Reefers pool.

Zain Al-Qaws -- **Government of The Republic of Iraq (Ministry of Agriculture & Agrarian Reform-State Fisheries Co), Iraq; Haugesund MV, Haugesund, 1979; 5061/6976gt, 9247dwt, 144m, 4ha, 8x5tn der, 11,400bhp Horten-Sulzer, 21kn. (Tolerton)**

Tuscan Star -- **Blue Star Line, UK; Drammen, 1972; 4905/6677gt, 9168dwt, 140m, 4ha, 8x5tn der, 14,850bhp Sulzer, 23kn. (Tolerton)**

The Drammen series ships flew a variety of ensigns, ranging from British like Blue Star's Glasgow-registered *Tuscan Star* (top), built in 1972 as the *Labrador Clipper*, to that of Morocco like the Casablanca-registered *Imilchil* of 1976 (centre). In all three ships were built for Morocco's Comanav. The first, the *Ifni*, shows the lines of the Drammen reefer to advantage (below) under later ownership as the *Brasilia Reefer*. She was the first of the later improved Drammens.

Imilchil -- **Compagnie Marocaine de Navigation, Morocco; Drammen, 1976; 7563gt, 9634dwt, 144m, 4ha, 8x5tn der, 13,200bhp Sulzer, 22.5kn. (Tolerton)**

Brasilia Reefer -- **Channel Maritime Co (International Reefer Services), Malta; Drammen, 1975; 7563gt, 9635dwt, 144m, 4ha, 8x5tn der, 13,199bhp Sulzer, 23.2kn. (Kees Lous)**

Bagno El Triunfo -- Elmshurst Shipping Ltd (Cool Ship Management), Panama; Framnaes, Sandefjord, 1975; 6702gt, 9147dwt, 140m, 4ha, 8x5tn der, 13,199bhp Horten-Sulzer, 23.25kn. (Tolerton)

One of the most imposing names in the series was carried by the *Bagno El Triunfo* (top), one of two ships built by Framnaes, both for East German state owner Deutsche Seereederei. The *Bagno El Triunfo* traded for DSR for 15 years as the *Heinrich Heine*, surviving a serious collision with an Indonesian ship in 1988.

Hamburg-Sud was among the prominent West European owners to operate a Drammen -- the Panamanian-flagged *Cap Frio* (centre), built in 1974 as the *Frigoartico*. She later traded as the *Tropical Sintra* (below) for Dole under the Liberian flag.

Cap Frio -- Star Determination Shipping Corp (Companhia Nacional de Navegacao), Panama; Drammen, 1974; 5426/7148gt, 9736dwt, 144m, 4ha, 8x5tn der, 13,200bhp Sulzer, 21kn. (Tolerton)

Tropical Sintra -- Talita Shipping Ltd (Dole Fresh Fruit International), Liberia; Drammen, 1974; 7060gt, 9736dwt. (author's collection)

Cardiff Clipper -- Abeyreuth Shipping Co & others (Whitco Marine Services), UK; Smith's Dock, Middlesbrough, 1973; 4938/6680gt, 9145dwt, 140m, 4ha, 8x5tn der, 14,850bhp Clark-Sulzer, 23kn. (World Ship Society)

Teesside Clipper -- Curtis Shipping Co & others (Worth West Shipping Co), UK; Smith's Dock, Middlesbrough, 1972; 4938/6680gt, 9145dwt, 140m, 4ha, 8x5tn der, 14,850bhp Clark-Sulzer, 23kn. (World Ship Society)

Eight Drammens, the 23kn "Clipper" series for Maritime Fruit Carriers, were built by Smith's Dock, Middlesbrough, starting with the *Edinburgh Clipper* of 1972. Cunard snapped up her and three others as low-mileage buys in 1976-77 during the MFC disposals. She became the *Alsatia*, and the other Cunard acquisitions were the *Cardiff Clipper* (top) which became the *Alaunia*, the *Teesside Clipper* (centre) which became the *Andria*, and the *Glasgow Clipper* (*Andania*). The *Cardiff Clipper/Alaunia* is pictured (bottom) later in her career as the Cypriot *Frio Bremen*.

Frio Bremen -- Mazatlan Shipping Co (Laskaridis Shipping), Cyprus; Smith's Dock, Middlesbrough, 1973; 19kn. (Tolerton)

Rio Esmeraldas **-- Flota Bananera Ecuatoriana, Ecuador; Drammen, 1979; 5065/6987gt, 9344dwt, 144m, 4ha, 8x5tn der, 11,400bhp Horten-Sulzer, 21kn. (Tolerton)**

The last four Drammens were built for Flota Bananera Ecuatoriana, a 99% Ecuadorian state-owned company, as the *Rio Esmeraldas* (1979), *Rio Chone* (1980), *Paquisha* (1981), and, from Kaldnes, *Rio Babahoyo* (1980). The US $52 million order was invaluable for Norway at a time when its shipbuilding industry was struggling, but the escalating loan debt caused great resentment in Ecuador, and 20 years after FBE sold the ships in 1987 for US $12 million to Transnave resolution to what had become a very sensitive issue was still being sought. The first of the quartet, the *Rio Esmeraldas*, is shown (above) in FBE colours, and (below) as the *Balboa Reefer*.

Balboa Reefer **-- Omega Shipping Co (International Reefer Services), Cyprus; 7141gt. (Kees Lous)**

Isla Pinta -- Transportes Navieros Ecuatorianos, Ecuador; Kaldnes, Tonsberg, 1980; 5064/6975gt, 9344dwt, 144m, 4ha, 8x5tn der, 11,400bhp Horten-Sulzer, 22kn. (Tolerton)

Emanuel B -- Rex Compania Naviera, Bahamas; Drammen, 1976; 5076/6993gt, 9612dwt, 144m, 4ha, 4x5tn cr, 13,200bhp Sulzer, 22kn. (Tolerton)

Another of the controversial Ecuadorian quartet and the only Drammen built by Kaldnes was the *Rio Babahoyo* of 1980. In 1988 she became the *Isla Pinta* (top), still Ecuadorian-owned and seen here on charter to Reefer Express Lines. She could carry 36 containers.

Drammen yard owner Peter Berg took several of the series for his own companies, including the *Emanuel B* (centre) of 1976. She was built as the *Emanuel* and renamed in 1985, and was on her fifth name as the Saudi-flagged *Tbreed VII* (bottom).

Tbreed VII -- Saudi Coldstorage Co, Saudi Arabia; 7215gt. (Kevin Moore)

Ragni Berg -- **P/R Reeferberg (Peter Y Berg), Norway; Drammen, 1978; 5064/6984gt, 9495dwt, 144m, 4ha, 8x5tn der, 11,400bhp Horten-Sulzer, 21kn. (Tolerton)**

Another ship built for Berg which had an interesting variety of names during her career was the *Ragni Berg* of 1978. She is pictured (above) in Berg's distinctive funnel colours, blue with a red band bordered by narrow white bands, and a houseflag on the red band, and later in Lauritzen colours as the *Bahamian Reefer* (below), still Norwegian-flagged but now registered in Oslo instead of Drammen, after initially being Bahamian flagged when she took the JL-style name. Note the stern anchor.

Bahamian Reefer -- **Sea Reefer, Norway. (Tolerton)**

Otrant Frigo -- **Mediteranska Plovidba, Yugoslavia. (Tolerton)**

The *Bahamian Reefer* was then sold to Yugoslav owner Mediteranska Plovidba at the end of 1988 as the *Otrant Frigo*, still operating in the Lauritzen reefer pool. She subsequently traded as the *Adriatic Trader, UB Polaris*, and *Tbreed III* before ending her career at Alang in 2003.

Brasilia Reefer **(Kevin Moore)**

End of the line for the Drammen-built *Brasilia Reefer* (originally the Moroccan *Ifni*), pictured sailing from Durban for Mumbai and demolition in 2000.

CHAPTER SEVEN

MARITIME FRUIT CARRIERS AND THE CORE SHIPS

Maritime Fruit Carriers of Haifa blazed a meteoric trail through the reefer shipping world in the 1970s, but long after it had faded its ships remained a hard "core" of the reefer trades.

MFC developed from a small Israeli fishing company which in the 1960s decided to expand with four reefers, capitalising on Israeli government grants for shipping citrus and Norwegian shipbuilding subsidies. Within 10 years of the delivery of its first ship, MFC, guided by Russian-born Mila Brener and Polish-born Ya'acov Meridor, had grown into an international shipping conglomerate with more than 40 reefers under primarily the Israeli, West German, and British flags and 15 tankers, many of them ULCCs.

It was a growth probably unprecedented in world shipping, but while most traditional shipping companies worked through one bank, MFC was involved with about 30, and most of the ships were financed on short-term loans. After the 1974 oil crisis the banks' confidence in MFC eroded, and a stampede started to get their money back.

MFC did not go into liquidation, but in December 1975 it announced its ships would stop operating because of arrests or the loss of crews through nonpayment of wages. During 1976 ships were sold off. Thirty of the 42 reefers were secured for operation with Salen Reefer Services -- Salen's own viability having been threatened by MFC's difficulties. Salen's SRS division had been created to cooperate with MFC when the latter's wildfire growth threatened to destabilize the reefer market, and in 1970 it hired on 15-year charters all 42 of MFC's reefers to double its fleet. When MFC hit the wall in late 1975 with the peak season for reefers starting, SRS paid millions of dollars in advance rentals to keep the ships running. However, MFC's fall led to it unsuccessfully suing Salen in the United States courts, alleging its rescue action had damaged the chances of MFC restructuring and that for political reasons Salen had collaborated with some banks to try to force MFC into bankruptcy.

The MFC shipwreck was not a surprise to many observers. Even "Time" magazine warned in March 1973 that Brener and Meridor could be in a predicament if demand for their ships suddenly declined. MFC "has built its flotilla on a thin money base: only $102 million of equity in a fleet that will soon be worth roughly $1.7 billion. Typically, Maritime covers the down payment on a ship out of government subsidy, leases the vessel while it is still being built, and takes out a mortgage loan to cover the remaining construction costs, with the lease as security."

The development of the MFC reefer fleet started with the ordering of four 8240gt, 147m, four hold ships from Norway -- the *Lemoncore* delivered in 1964 from Bergens, followed by in 1965 by the *Mangocore* and *Avocadocore* from Akers, Oslo, and the *Bananacore* from Bergen. The quartet was Israeli-flagged and directly MFC-owned, and reputedly with the forecastle strengthened for a gun to be mounted. The "core" names characteristic of MFC came from the Hebrew word for cold.

MFC followed up with orders for 12 more ships to this design -- the *Persimmoncore* (1968), *Guavacore* (1969), *Anonacore* (1970), *Pecan* (1971) from Nylands, Oslo, and the *Tangerinecore* (1968), *Mandarincore* (1968), *Nectarinecore* (1970), *Satsumacore* (1970), *Navelinacore* (1970), *Sultanacore* (1970), and *Clementina* (1971) from Bergens, and *Sabracore* (1968) from Akers.

Slightly larger at 155m, and with five holds instead of four, was a class of six similar-looking ships -- the *Cherry* (1971), *Orange* (1972), *Maranga* (1972), *Cantaloup* (1973), *Tangelo* (1974) from Nylands and the *Morillo* (1971) from Bergens.

It's possibly a tribute to the reputation of the Aker ships that after the great MFC sell-off, many retained their names for many years under new ownership, although frequently with the "core" suffix deleted. Two, the *Navelinacore* and *Sultana*, were converted in the early 1980s to fruit juice tankers, having seven tanks installed to carry shipments of Brazilian orange juice.

As well as several of the early Drammen standard reefers built in Norway, MFC also commissioned all eight of the Drammen "Clipper" ships built by Smith's Dock, Middlesbrough, (see The Drammen Reefers chapter) in a 25 million pound order. These ships were completed in 1972-1974, and in the MFC disposals four were snapped up by the Cunard Line, which at this time was diversifying into reefer shipping and bulk carriers. Cunard also acquired the Nylands-built *Orange* and *Cantaloup*, renamed *Carmania* and *Carinthia* respectively, in 1976.

That year Cunard also swooped for what might be regarded as the jewels in the MFC crown -- the four largest ships. *Orchidea*, *Gladiola*, *Iris Queen* (all 1972), and *Chrysantema* (1973), built by Aalborg Vaerft, were renamed *Servia*, *Saxonia*, *Scythia*, and *Samaria* respectively. These 12,000gt ships were 175m long, with five holds and 16,356 cu/m insulated capacity. All four had long lay-ups in Vittoria Dock, Birkenhead, before being sold in 1985 along with *Carmania* and *Carinthia* to Greek reefer operator Kappa Maritime. Pleasing though it had been to see the Cunard names revived, it was not the same with their livery -- they invariably operated in charterers' funnel colours and with gray hulls.

Saxonia was one of the merchant ships requisitioned and modified as a stores ship at the end of the Falklands war. *Scythia* chalked up rather less memorable milestones, with major engineroom fires both during her Cunard career, in 1976 on passage from Falmouth to Casablanca, and as the Cypriot-flag *Centaurus* at Wilmington, Delaware, in 1989 which led to her being declared a constructive total loss. Indeed misadventure contributed to the demise of three of the four, with -- under later ownership -- the *Saxonia* and *Servia* likewise being declared CTLs after collision and fire respectively.

As well as Cunard, notable beneficiaries of the disposal of MFC's fleet were United Fruit and Hamburg operator Frigomaris, which appeared to have a connection to MFC and was taken over by Ganymed Shipping in 1977. A curiosity of some of the German ex-MFC ships was that although registered in Hamburg they flew the Panamanian flag.

Core class (147m, four hatch)
From Bergens, Bergen:
449 - 1964 *Lemoncore*, *Omoa* 76, to Shanghai for b/u 85.
450 - 1965 *Bananacore*, *Chaiten* 76, to Kaohsiung for b/u 84.
463 - 1968 *Mandarincore*, *Ceiba* 76, *Chillan* 79, to Chittagong for b/u 93.
464 - 1968 *Tangerinecore*, *Condata* 76, *Lucky* 88, to Alang for b/u 93.
636 - 1970 *Nectarinecore*, *Nectarine* 75, *Valiant Reefer* 88, *Milos Reefer* 89, aground off Glory of Russia Cape, St Matthew Island, voyage Houston-Tokyo and abandoned 89.
637 - 1970 *Satsumacore*, *Satsuma* 75, *Copacabana Reefer* 88, fire while loading cotton Piraeus 93 and to Aliaga for b/u.
638 - 1970 *Navelinacore*, *Navelina* 75, *Pasadena* 76, *Pasadena I* 81, *Ouro do Brasil* 82, *Citrus do Brasil* 92, to India for b/u 03.
639 - 1970 *Sultana* (launched as *Sultanacore*), *Ariane I* 76, *Sol do Brasil* 84, *Suco do Brasil* 94, to Alang for b/u 02.
648 - 1971 *Clementina*, to Alang for b/u 03.
From Nylands, Oslo:
603 - 1968 *Persimmoncore*, *Condora* 77, *Frio Adriatic* 87, to Alang for b/u 94.
608 - 1969 *Guavacore*, *Guava* 74, *Rosemary* 80, *Bassro Freezer* 85, *Frio Antarctic* 85, to Chittagong for b/u 93.
609 - 1970 *Anonacore*, *Anona* 74, *Ananas* 86, *Anona* 86 *Venture Reefer* 88, *Kassos Reefer* 88, *Chios Reefer* 91, to Alang for b/u 94.
647 - 1971 *Pecan*, *Hispaniola* 84, *Pecan* 85, to Alang for b/u 01.
From Akers, Oslo:
557 - 1965 *Mangocore*, *Olancho* 76, to Lianyungang for b/u 85.
559 - 1965 *Avocadocore*, *Orica* 76, to Kaohsiung for b/u 85.
602 - 1968 *Sabracore*, *Corinto* 76, *Cholguan* 79, *Zante Reefer* 87, *Frozen Lulis* 89, to Alang for b/u 89.

Super Core class (155m, five hatch)
From Bergens, Bergen:
649 - 1971 *Morillo*,
From Nylands, Oslo:
650 - 1971 *Cherry*, *Cayman* 84, *R P Cayman* 87, *Cherry* 96.
652 - 1972 *Orange*, *Carmania* 76, *Perseus* 85, to Alang for b/u 99.
654 - 1972 *Maranga*, *Brunsland* 76, *Tropical Land* 78, *Rio Guayas* 86, *Tropical Land* 97.
655 - 1973 *Cantaloup*, *Carinthia* 76, *Pegasus* 86, *Star Light* 94, *Pelagos* 95, to Alang for b/u 00.
656 - 1974 *Tangelo*, *Atlantic Ocean* 76, *Republica del Ecuador* 86, *Irish Sea* 95, aground Bedwell Island voyage Buenos Aires-Puerto Bolivar in ballast 99, and to Alang for b/u 00.

12,000 gt, 175m, five hatch class, from Aalborg Vaerft, Aalborg:
195 - 1972 *Gladiola*, *Saxonia* 76, *Carina* 86, seriously damaged in collision off Ostend, voyage Bellingham-Flushing, 95, to Aliaga for b/u 96.
196 - 1972 *Orchidea*, *Servia* 76, *Castor* 85, *Kastora* 87, fire voyage Puerto Limon-New Orleans 89, to Gadani Beach for b/u 90.
197 - 1972 *Iris Queen*, *Scythia* 76, *Centaurus* 85, fire at Wilmington 89, to Chittagong for b/u 89.
198 - 1973 *Chrysantema*, *Samaria* 76, *Capricorn* 86, to Alang for b/u 99.

Avocadocore -- **Maritime Fruit Carriers, Israel; Akers, Oslo, 1965; 5955/8243gt, 8535dwt, 147m, 4ha, 12x5-10der, 11,500bhp Akers-B&W, 20kn. (Trevor Jones)**

One of the original Maritime Fruit Carriers ships, the *Avocadocore* of 1965, during her Israeli-flagged MFC days and in Salen funnel colours (above). In 1976 she was one of several Cores bought by United Fruit and operated in its Honduran-flag subsidiary Empresa Hondurena de Vapores as the *Orica*. With their sturdy goalpost masts the Cores were not as elegant as some contemporary reefers, but most gave very long service in the reefer trades. Another of the basic 147m, four hatch Core reefers was the *Anona* of 1970 (below), built as the *Anonacore* for MFC. As the *Anona* owned by Intermare KG, she was registered in Hamburg but flew the flag of Panama.

Anona -- **Intermare KG, KS Kuhlschiff GmbH & Co (Christian Ahrenkiel), Panama; Nylands, Oslo, 1970; 5902/8191gt, 9876dwt, 147m, 4ha, 2x5-15 & 8x5-10der, 11,500bhp Nylands-B&W, 19kn. (Tolerton)**

Nectarine **-- Intermare KG, KS Kuhlschiff GmbH & Co (Christian Ahrenkiel), Panama; Bergens, Bergen, 1970; 5901/8190gt, 10,252dwt, 147m, 4ha, 2x15, 4x10, & 4x5tn der, 11,500bhp Akers-B&W, 19kn. (Tolerton)**

The *Nectarinecore* was another 1970 MFC completion to later operate for Intermare. She became the *Nectarine* (above), again Hamburg-registered, Panamanian-flagged, and chartered to Salen. Two other 1970 completions, the *Navelinacore* and *Sultanacore*, were converted to fruit juice carriers later in their careers, the former becoming the *Ouro do Brasil* in 1982 and then renamed *Citrus do Brasil* (below) in 1992 to free the former name for a new vessel.

Citrus do Brasil **-- MV Pasadena Shipping Corp (Maritime Services Aleuropa GmbH), Liberia; Bergens, Bergen, 1970; 147m, 1 ta & 6 wing ta, 11,500bhp Akers-B&W, 19kn. (author's collection)**

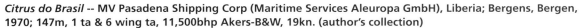

Pecan -- **County Maritime Corp (Frigomaris Shipping), Panama; Nylands, Oslo, 1971; 6172/8068gt, 9876dwt, 147m, 4ha, 2x15tn & 8x10tn der, 11,500bhp Nylands-B&W, 19.5kn. (Tolerton)**

Two more of MFC's standard Cores, both from Nylands, to find their way into Hamburg ownership were the *Pecan* (top) of 1971 and *Rosemary* (centre) of 1969, which was previously the *Guava* and *Guavacore*. A distinctive mustard paint for the hulls seemed to be a feature of most of the German-owned Cores. The *Anona* illustrated earlier became the Greek *Kassos Reefer* (bottom) in 1988, chartered to Lauritzen. All these ships had four sidedoors, port and starboard.

Rosemary -- **Rosemary Shipping Co SA (Ganymed Schiffahrtsgesellschaft mbH), Panama; Nylands, Oslo, 1969; 6198/8065gt, 10,252dwt, 147m, 4ha, 2x15 & 8x5-10tn der, 11,500bhp Nylands-B&W, 19kn. (Tolerton)**

Kassos Reefer -- **Mota Compania Naviera SA (Transcontinental Maritime & Trading SA), Greece. (Tolerton)**

Clementina -- **Pro Line Ltd & Co GmbH (Ganymed Shipping), Burma; Bergens, Bergen, 1971; 5683/8067gt, 9750dwt, 147m, 4ha, 2x15 & 8x5-10tn der, 10,500bhp Nylands-B&W, 20kn. (Tolerton)**

Two more of the German MFC/Frigomaris ships – the Core *Clementina* (above) and the Super Core *Cayman* (below), completed as the *Cherry* and the first of the five Super Cores built by Nylands. The *Clementina*, which went to Alang in 2003 for demolition, was the only standard Core to carry her name unchanged during her career. The *Cayman* clearly shows the transom stern of the Super Cores.

Cayman -- **Reefer Pacific Ganymed Schiffahrts GmbH & Co (Ganymed), Panama; Nylands, Oslo, 1971; 7355/9524gt, 10,800dwt, 155m, 5ha, 2x15 & 12x5-10tn der, 17,400bhp Nylands-B&W, 22kn. (Tolerton)**

Tangelo -- **Glasszoon Ltd & Heronchoice Ltd, UK; Nylands, Oslo, 1974; 7330/9749gt, 10,973dwt, 155m, 5ha, 2x15 & 12x5-10tn der, 17,400bhp Nylands-B&W, 21.5kn. (World Ship Society)**

From 1971 to 1974 MFC added six Super Core ships, 155m long with five hatches and side doors port and starboard for each hold, to the fleet. They also had three goalpost masts and more powerful machinery than their predecessors. Fuel consumption was about 63tn a day. The last was the *Tangelo* (above) which was sold in 1976 to become the Liberian *Atlantic Ocean* and then in 1986 became Ecuadorian owner Naviera del Pacifico's *Republica del Ecuador* (below). By this time she had also been modified to carry 189 containers.

Republica del Ecuador -- **Naviera del Pacifico (Ecuadorian Line), Ecuador; 7245/9618gt. (Tolerton)**

Morillo -- **Trans Malayan Shipping Inc (Ganymed Shipping GmbH), Philippines; Bergens, Bergen, 1971; 6865/9592gt, 10,800dwt, 155m, 5ha, 2x15 & 12x5-10tn der, 17,399bhp Nylands-B&W, 22kn. (Tolerton)**

The first Super Cores were the *Morillo* (above) and *Cherry* of 1971, acquired that year by Frigomaris (which seemed to emerge flourishing from the wreckage of MFC), and the largest German reefers at that time. The former was the only Super Core built by Bergens, while Nylands built the other five. The *Morillo* was still in service in 2007 and, uniquely among the Super Cores, still under her original name. She is pictured in the 1990s operating for Seatrade.

Samaria -- **The Cunard Steam-Ship Co (Cunard Shipping Services), UK; Aalborg Vaerft, Aalborg, 1973; 8577/12,059gt, 12,180dwt, 175m, 5ha, 2x15tn & 12x5tn der, 23,200bhp B&W, 23.5kn. (Tolerton)**

The largest and most powerful reefers for MFC were four 12,000gt ships concluding with the *Chrysantema* of 1973, pictured as the *Samaria* and chartered by Salen after she and her three sisters were acquired by Cunard. Built by Aalborg, they were 175m long, five hatch vessels with sidedoors port and starboard for all five holds.

Apollonian Grace -- Apollonian Grace Co SA, Greece; Aalborg Vaerft, Aalborg, 1958; 4717gt, 5791dwt, 132m, 4ha, 8x5tn der, 8100bhp 2xB&W, 18kn. (Tolerton)

Still operating for Lauritzen but now with a green hull instead of red -- the *Apollonian Grace*, formerly the *Belgian Reefer* of 1958, and sold with charter back in 1973.

CHAPTER EIGHT

J LAURITZEN

In May 1932 the small coal-fired steamer *Ulla* sailed from the Helsingor shipyard in Denmark for Fort de France in the French West Indies. Shipowner Ditlev Lauritzen and his sons Ivar and Knud no doubt watched her departure with more than a little anxiety, for the Ulla was sailing into uncharted waters for their business, and represented a significant gamble.

The *Ulla* had been delivered only the previous September from the Helsingor yard as a conventional 1564gt, 12kn cargo ship. However, she soon returned to Helsingor for installation of an Atlas ammonia cooling plant as J Lauritzen's first refrigerated ship, the first of six sister ships to have a cooling plant fitted for them to carry fruit.

The *Ulla* successfully carried her cargo of bananas to Le Havre -- and the foundation for a great shipping success story had been laid. Lauritzen's pioneer fruitships had a major drawback -- the bunker capacity was inadequate for the passages to load in the West Indies and West Africa, and coal had to be carried on deck. It was no doubt to the enormous relief of Lauritzen's seamen as well as the pride of the management that only two years after the first reefer sailing of the *Ulla* that the company's first refrigerated motorships *Asta* and *Dora* (both sold to French owners the next year) were delivered from Burmeister & Wain, followed by a third from Helsingor in 1935. This ship, the 1862gt *Pacific Reefer*, quickly renamed *Yrsa* and then *African Reefer*, was to sail successfully for 28 years -- the first in a dynasty of successful and often innovative refrigerated motorship designs through to the world's biggest reefer, the *Ditlev Lauritzen* launched in August, 1990, at the Lauritzen-owned Danyard, Frederikshavn. In contrast to the 3000 cu/m insulated capacity of the *Ulla*, the 1990 giant offered 20,894 cu/m.

Probably no other shipping company has been successful in as many spheres of shipowning as the Lauritzen group. JL has been prominent in bulk shipping, gas and oil tankers, heavylift shipping, offshore drilling, and, briefly, cruise shipping, and been ice masters through its unique involvement in polar shipping at both ends of the world. Through DFDS it has also been to the fore with passenger ferries and general cargo shipping. However, it is reefer shipping for which Lauritzen is most famous. The red-hulled JL reefers (the colour was originally adopted for the polar vessels) were familiar in all parts of the world, and while other reefer operators came and went, Lauritzen maintained its eminence for more than 70 years in this very specialised area before bowing out in 2007.

Copenhagen-based, the company was founded by Ditlev Lauritzen in 1884 in the west Jutland port of Esbjerg. It remained the traditional port of registry as the JL fleet grew. World War Two undermined the successful start Lauritzen had made in reefer shipping in the '30s, and it finished the war with only four reefers -- fortunately for it, all modern motorships.

Reefer fleet renewal began with the addition of the *Mexican Reefer* (1953) from Helsingor, and *Brazilian Reefer* (1953) and *Peruvian Reefer* (1954) from Aalborg, all 3947gt, 18kn twin-screw motorships with the characteristic streamlining of Scandinavian ships of this era. Their speed and innovations like more fire-resistant aluminium-lined fibreglass insulation instead of cork and wood made them state of the art. Employed primarily in the banana trades, the three ships were sold, curiously, to Lauritzen's big rival Salen in 1963, but sold again the next year to the Soviet Union, where they had long careers as fish carriers. They were followed by the slightly larger 4900gt, 18.5kn *Arabian Reefer* (1957), *Belgian Reefer* (1958), *Chilean Reefer* (1959), and *Ecuadorian Reefer* (1962) from Aalborg, also twin-screw ships, and able to carry cargo at down to minus 20deg C.

These ships were followed by another notable class, the six-ship *Italian Reefer* series from Lauritzen's Aalborg yard. Quite different in appearance from the previous seven, these 22.5kn ships had their names painted in large letters amidships on the hull. And for observers too far away to read them, the three-quarter aft profile, tall tapering funnel, Velle derricks, transom stern, and a prominent stern house which incorporated a swimming pool combined to make any ship of this class instantly recognisable. In service in 1968, the *Italian Reefer* was followed by the *Nippon Reefer* (1969), *Persian Reefer* (1970, diplomatically renamed *Peruvian Reefer* in 1981), *Roman Reefer* (1970), *Samoan Reefer* (1973), and *Tunisian Reefer* (1974). The three forward holds had four decks and the aft hold three, with a total capacity of 12,660 cu/m. Like their predecessors, the ships were technically advanced for their day, and had bridge control of the main engines and unmanned engineroom. The *Italian Reefer* and *Nippon Reefer* were sold in 1978, but the latter four operated for JL for more than 20 years, the *Samoan Reefer* and *Tunisian Reefer* being lengthened by a new 20.5m cargo section at Jurong in 1988.

During the course of this class's introduction, Lauritzen joined forces with another shipping giant, P&O, to set up Lauritzen-Peninsular Reefers in 1971, when P&O was diversifying into tramp reefers. The pool's chartered ships operated with a red funnel with three white triangles in a stylized "LPR." The partnership lasted until May 1983 when P&O relinquished its holding after selling its four Drammen reefers to the Sembawang group of Singapore, and JL relaunched its reefer division as Lauritzen Reefers.

By this time Lauritzen had introduced a new quartet of owned ships. At 144m long, the *Asian Reefer* and *Balkan Reefer* of 1978 from Japan's Hayashikane Shipbuilding and the *Canadian Reefer* (1979) and *Ecuadorian Reefer* (1980) from Aalborg were the same length as the *Italian Reefer* class and with some external resemblance, but beamier with greater cargo capacity, around 16,600 cu/m. All four holds had four decks, and there were separate small banana hatches on the weather deck. Twenty-two knot ships, they had the accommodation block set just forward of the engineroom and funnel to minimise noise and vibration. On her maiden voyage the *Asian Reefer* carried New Zealand apples to Europe and soon after brought cartoned citrus fruit from Cape Town and Port Elizabeth to Marseilles, Antwerp, and Cardiff before employment carrying bananas for United Brands from Central and South America to European and US east and west coast ports.

Lauritzen kept its fleet in the van of reefer operations by regular upgrading with both owned and chartered ships, and early in the 1980s added three of the world's largest engines-aft refrigerated ships, the 142m, 8012gt *Nippon Reefer* and *New Zealand Reefer* of 1982 from Kyokuyo Shipbuilding and similar *Reefer Tiger* of 1983 from Hayashikane off the stocks on long term charters. All three met the developing requirement for carrying palletised cargo. By now the virtue of engines aft vessels in enhancing carrying capacity on a given hull length was becoming apparent in reefer shipping as it had long been in oil and dry bulk shipping, and considerably larger examples were on the drawing boards at companies like Lauritzen. Aesthetically the results were not so attractive as the traditional reefers, although one exception was perhaps another Lauritzen charter acquisition at this time, the 6127gt *Reefer Penguin* of 1983 from Shikoku Dockyard, at

145m an exceptionally fine lined vessel and fractionally longer than the *Asian Reefer*. On her maiden voyage the *Reefer Penguin* sailed to Timaru and loaded lamb carcasses for Jeddah, then loaded palletised apples in Tasmania for Helsinki, Helsingborg, and Drammen.

Lauritzen introduced its first ULRC (ultra large reefer carrier) with the 12,383gt *Anne B*, built for the Lauritzen pool by Norwegian owner Finn Bugge, in 1983 from Hashihama Zosen. The ULRCs lacked any resemblance to the elegant reefers of the past, but were to set new records for cargo carrying while at the same time offering economic operation with more fuel-efficient engines. An 18kn ship, the *Anne B* was 144m long and had 17,840 cu m of cargo space in four near box-shaped holds served by four 10tn cranes. She could carry 6200 pallets and 152 containers on deck. Fuel consumption was 28tn a day. The *Anne B* was followed by the *Betty B* from the same yard (both quickly set world records for pallet cargoes carrying South African deciduous fruit), while Hyundai completed four very similar ships, the *Australian Reefer*, *African Reefer*, *Reefer Jambu*, and *American Reefer*, in 1984-85.

Two ships of similar size, the *Anglian Reefer* and *Argentinean Reefer*, both from Hashihama, were added in 1988. At 14,932dwt the *Anglian Reefer* was the world's largest reefer when she went into service, and carried a record cargo of 334,000 cartons of New Zealand apples and pears from Napier to Antwerp on her first voyage. Her sister promptly emulated her with a record cargo of palletised kiwifruit from Tauranga to Antwerp.

Within a short time the record for the biggest reefers was bettered again by Lauritzen, with the four 20kn ships of the *Ditlev Lauritzen* class from Danyard, Frederikshavn. The 14,406gt, 16,600dwt lead ship, delivered in September 1990, was followed by the *Ivar Lauritzen* later in the year and *Knud Lauritzen* and *Jorgen Lauritzen* in 1991. Developed in collaboration with the Danish Ministry of Industry's Project Ship programme, the *Ditlev Lauritzen* was 164m long with a capacity of 20,894 cu/m -- the volume of 150,000 domestic fridges -- in five holds. These were served by three 36tn and two 8tn cranes, and she could carry 7000 pallets. She had full container capacity below deck and in total could carry 480 TEUs (236 below deck and 244 on the weather deck and the hatch covers) or 224 40ft containers (104 below deck). The 23 cargo compartments had individual cooling plants and could be divided into nine sections for different cargoes, and at temperatures down to minus 29deg C. The engine was a 15,288bhp B&W from Korea Heavy Industries, and the ship had bow and stern thrusters and a controllable pitch propeller. The Project Ship programme envisaged a crew of only six for these giant reefers, so of necessity they were technically very sophisticated ships. Interestingly, as a nod to the US $200m quartet's private investors, the ships were registered at different ports -- the *Ditlev* at the traditional JL home of Esbjerg, the *Ivar* at Aabenraa, the *Knud* at Frederikshavn, and the *Jorgen* at Ribe.

Lauritzen rounded off the programme of very large reefer construction with a 10,200gt, 19kn chartered pair from Shin Kurushima, the *Uruguayan Reefer* of 1993 and *Mexican Reefer* of 1994, both flagged in Panama. The former's first commercial voyage was a little unusual -- she carried 6700tn of bagged peanuts (worth, at US$6m, hardly peanuts) from Qingdao to Flushing.

The Lauritzen pool was also augmented in 1992 by five very fast (22kn), medium-size 7900gt reefers, the *Bothnian Reefer*, *Carelian Reefer*, *Lapponian Reefer*, *Savonian Reefer*, and *Scandinavian Reefer* from Kvaerner and Kaldnes. Larger versions of the Erikson 5000gt "Penguin" series (see page 141), they were, inevitably, dubbed the "Emperor Penguins." Their ownership has been a complicated story, but the *Carelian Reefer*, *Lapponian Reefer*, and *Savonian Reefer* were all originally operated by Erikson before the Finnish company quit the pool, and all except the *Bothnian Reefer* were to come under Lauritzen ownership, with the *Scandinavian Reefer* a JL ship from the start.

At the end of 2000 Lauritzen announced the acquisition of its big rival Cool Carriers from Norwegian owner Leif Hoegh for US$35.4 million, taking effect on January 1, 2001. The change did not involve any vessel purchases. The new LauritzenCool was to be headquartered in Stockholm and ranked as the world's largest operator of specialised reefers.

Further rationalisation among the reefer shipping giants in 2005 saw LauritzenCool and NYK Reefers merge their reefer operations as NYKLauritzenCool, run from Stockholm, with a fleet of more than 70 reefers, most of them with significant container capacity. However, in August 2007 it was announced that NYK Reefers had acquired the Lauritzen shares. Thus after three-quarters of a century, reefer shipping lost perhaps its most famous name, Lauritzen deciding instead to concentrate on its bulker and tanker interests.

The *Ecuadorian Reefer* of 1962. (Tolerton)

Arabian Reefer class, from Aalborg Vaerft, Aalborg:
106 - 1957 *Arabian Reefer, Apollonian Champion* 73, *Ocean Freezer* 77, to Bombay for b/u 80.
108 - 1958 *Belgian Reefer, Apollonian Grace* 73, *Atlantic Freezer* 77, to Gadani Beach
for b/u 81.
121 - 1959 *Chilean Reefer, Union Reefer* 77, to Chittagong for b/u 83.
122 - 1962 *Ecuadorian Reefer, Fair Reefer* 78, to El Ferrol for b/u 84.

Italian Reefer class, from Aalborg Vaerft, Aalborg:
177 - 1968 *Italian Reefer, Arctic Ocean* 78, *Bonita* 84, *Arabian Sea* 95, seriously damaged by fire, Guayaquil River 00, to Alang for b/u 01.
178 - 1970 *Nippon Reefer, Indian Ocean* 78, *Provincia de Los Rios* 84 (lengthened 91),
Celtic Sea 95.
182 - 1970 *Persian Reefer, Peruvian Reefer* 81, aground off Malmo voyage Copenhagen-Riga 90, *Orange Reefer* 92, to Alang for b/u 01.
183 - 1970 *Roman Reefer, Mango Reefer* 92, to Alang for b/u 99.
201 - 1973 *Samoan Reefer* (lengthened 88), *Arctic Swan* 95, *Arctic Night* 02, to Chittagong for b/u 07.
202 - 1974 *Tunisian Reefer* (lengthened 88), *Arctic Goose* 95, *Arctic Ice* 02, to Chittagong for b/u 07.

Asian Reefer class
From Hayashikane Shipbuilding, Nagasaki:
863 - 1978 Asian Reefer, Baltic Sky 02.
864 - 1978 Balkan Reefer, Baltic Sun 02.
From Aalborg Vaerft, Aalborg:
225 - 1979 Canadian Reefer, Canadian Star 01, Baltic Snow 01.
226 - 1980 Ecuadorian Reefer (was to have been named *Egyptian Reefer*), *Baltic Stream 01.*

14,000dwt class
From Hashihama Zosen, Tadotsu:
825 - 1983 Anne B, Belgian Reefer 92.
826 - 1984 Betty B, Brazilian Reefer 92.
From Hyundai, Ulsan:
289 - 1984 Australian Reefer, Rauma Reefer 00, Ice Runner 06.
287 - 1985 Reefer Jambu, Ice Rose 96.
288 - 1985 American Reefer, Ice River 96.
290 - 1985 African Reefer, Ice Ranger 00.
From Hashihama Zosen, Tadotsu:
859 - 1988 Anglian Reefer, Parana 03.
860 - 1988 Argentinean Reefer, Amazonas 03.

Family class, from Danyard, Frederikshavn:
702 - 1990 Ditlev Lauritzen.
703 - 1990 Ivar Lauritzen.
704 - 1991 Knud Lauritzen.
705 - 1991 Jorgen Lauritzen.

11,000dwt class
From Kvaerner Kleven Ulsteinvik, Ulsteinvik:
243 - 1992 (hull from Kaldnes, Tonsberg) *Lapponian Reefer.*
244 - 1992 (hull from Tangen Verft, Kragero, & completed Langsten, Tomrefjord) *Carelian Reefer,*
Chilean Reefer 97, bottom damage when struck breakwater Abidjan 99.
246 - 1992 (from KK Leirvik) *Scandinavian Reefer.*
247 - 1992 (hull from Tangen, completed Langsten) *Savonian Reefer, Peruvian Reefer 97.*
248 - 1992 (hull from Kaldnes, Tonsberg) *Bothnian Reefer, Wellington Star 03.*

11,500dwt class, from Shin Kurushima, Akitsu:
2780 - 1993 Uruguayan Reefer, Fortune Bay 99, Fortuna Bay 03.
2781 - 1994 Mexican Reefer, Mexican Bay 06

The *Brazilian Reefer* (ex-*Betty B* of 1984). (Tolerton)

African Reefer -- J Lauritzen, Denmark; Helsingors, Helsingor, 1935; 1862gt, 2420dwt, 96m, 1800bhp B&W, 13.75kn. (J Lauritzen)

Few reefers have given longer service to one owner than Lauritzen's pioneer *African Reefer* (above), launched in 1935 as the *Pacific Reefer*, then into service as the *Yrsa* before being renamed *African Reefer* in 1936. She went to Dutch shipbreakers in 1963. The first of a series of similar ships for JL, she was also the first to become familiar in New Zealand ports, where the company was to have such an enormous presence in later decades. She was closely followed into service by the *Canadian Reefer* (below). Her career was much shorter -- she was torpedoed by a U boat off Cape Finisterre in 1940.

Canadian Reefer -- Vesterhavet (J Lauritzen), Denmark; Nakskov Skibsvaerft, Nakskov, 1936; 1831gt, 2400dwt, 89m, 1800bhp B&W, 13.75kn. (J Lauritzen)

Another view of the *African Reefer* near the end of her career (top), now with the red hull. Lauritzen adopted this in the 1950s as a point of difference for the fleet after using it for the polar vessel *Kista Dan*. Another of the early Lauritzen motor reefers was the *Argentinean Reefer*, launched at Aalborg in 1940 but laid up during the war. In 1968 she was bought by New Zealand's Union Steam Ship Co for its trade to the Pacific Islands and renamed *Taveuni*, and is pictured laid up in Auckland before being sold for a voyage to breakers in Taiwan. (*African Reefer* photo, APN; *Taveuni* photos, Andy Copping)

The twin-screw *Chilean Reefer* of 1959 (below) was one of the distinctive ships from the group's own Aalborg shipyard which modernised the fleet during reconstruction in the 1950s.

Chilean Reefer -- **J Lauritzen, Denmark; Aalborg Vaerft, Aalborg, 1959; 4981gt, 5790dwt, 132m, 4ha, 8x5tn der, 8100bhp 2xB&W, 18kn. (Tolerton)**

Arctic Ocean -- **Naviera del Pacifico SA, Ecuador; Aalborg Vaerft, Aalborg, 1968; 5978gt, 8636dwt, 145m, 4ha, 4x5tn der, 15,000bhp B&W, 22.5kn. (Tolerton)**

The six ships of the *Italian Reefer* class completed at JL's Aalborg Vaerft yard in 1968-1974 were reefers of unique appearance that gave JL excellent service. Although only six years separated the introduction of the last of the 1957-62 quartet, the *Ecuadorian Reefer*, and the arrival of the first of the new class, they were considerably larger and their appearance could not have been more different. The first two, *Italian Reefer* and *Nippon Reefer* of 1968 and 1969 respectively, were sold in 1978 as the *Arctic Ocean* and *Indian Ocean*, and the former was transferred four years later to Ecuadorian owner Naviera del Pacifico with whose blue funnel and a traditional white reefer hull instead of Lauritzen red she is pictured (above). The six vessels of this class were registered at Esbjerg, the small Jutland port where the company originated, but the *Roman Reefer* of 1970 is pictured (below) later in her career operating for JL's Nassau subsidiary Frigg Shipping. Transfers of this sort seemed to be accompanied by a change to a duller red paint scheme than the bright red of the Danish-flag vessels.

Roman Reefer -- **Frigg Shipping, Bahamas; Aalborg Vaerft, Aalborg, 1970; 6010gt, 8941dwt, 145m, 4ha, 4x5tn der, 15,000 B&W, 20kn. (Tolerton)**

Peruvian Reefer -- Frigg Shipping Ltd (J Lauritzen A/S), Bahamas; Aalborg Vaerft, Aalborg, 1970; 6010gt, 8941dwt, 145m, 4ha, 4x5tn der, 15,000bhp B&W, 22.5kn. (Tolerton)

The *Persian Reefer* also of 1970 received the more PC name of *Peruvian Reefer* (above) in 1981, and on her first voyage after renaming carried eggs, grapes, and apples from Port Hueneme and Seattle to Sharjah. The prominent stern house of this class incorporated a swimming pool. The last two of the class were the *Samoan Reefer* of 1973 and the *Tunisian Reefer* (below) of 1974. These two were lengthened by 20m at Jurong, Singapore in 1988, the alteration incorporating a 10tn crane and an additional hatch.

Tunisian Reefer -- J Lauritzen A/S, Denmark; Aalborg Vaerft, Aalborg, 1974; 5915gt, 8941dwt, 144m, 4ha, 4x5tn der, 15,000bhp B&W, 22.5kn. (Tolerton)

***Ecuadorian Reefer* -- J Lauritzen A/S, Denmark; Aalborg Vaerft, Aalborg, 1980; 8849gt, 12,570dwt, 144m, 8ha (4ho), 6x5tn cr, 14,966bhp Helsingor-B&W, 22kn. (Author's collection)**

The next class of ships, the *Asian Reefer* and *Balkan Reefer* (1978) from Hayashikane and the *Canadian Reefer* (1979) and, pictured above, *Ecuadorian Reefer* (1980) from Aalborg were all to give Lauritzen long service. With basically the same overall length as their predecessor class, they were much better cargo carriers.

Their speed meant they frequently operated as banana ships, although some representative voyages of the *Balkan Reefer* in 1979 were typical of their trading: Florida, citrus, and Ecuador, bananas, for New Zealand; New Zealand, meat and onions, for Japan and Korea; ballast to New Zealand; Timaru and Napier, sheep and lamb carcasses for the Black Sea.

Incidentally, an examination of voyages for Lauritzen ships quickly shows reefer trading is more than just bananas, citrus and deciduous, and meat and dairy products -- and vehicles for back voyages or off-season. The *Canadian Reefer* loaded rolls of newsprint in 1980 in St John, New Brunswick, for Ecuador, and in 1993 the *Argentinean Reefer* loaded baled cotton in Nacala, Mozambique, and Pemba, Tanzania, and cotton in containers at Dar es Salaam, Tanzania, for Leixoes, Portugal. In the 1983-84 winter, the *Tunisian Reefer*, *Peruvian Reefer*, and *Roman Reefer* all carried tobacco from Turkey, Yugoslavia, and Greece to Richmond, Virginia. Chestnuts for the US Thanksgiving and Christmas celebrations have sometimes been a cargo, the *African Reefer*, *Southern Universal*, and *Colombian Reefer* all being placed to load in Salerno for Philadelphia in 1986. Some other unusual voyages: *American Reefer*, onions, Mumbai to Novorossiysk, 1995; *Chilean Reefer*, tuna, Victoria, Seychelles, to Bangkok, 1988; *Argentinean Reefer*, *Jorgen Lauritzen*, *Knud Lauritzen*, feta cheese, Esbjerg to Bandar Khomeini, 1991; *Anne B*, grapes, Limassol to Dover, 1984; *Nippon Reefer*, palletised garlic, Lanshantou, China, to US east coast, 1992.

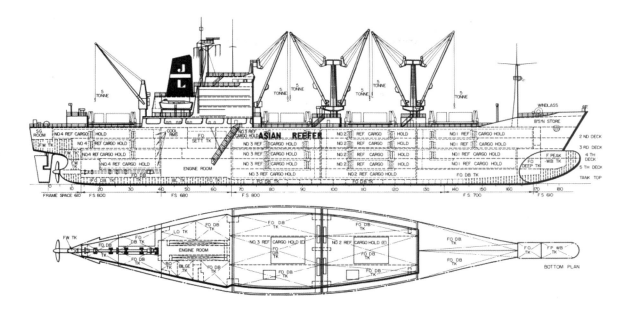

Asian Reefer, the first of this class. J Lauritzen A/S, Denmark; Hayashikane Shipbuilding, Nagasaki, 1978; 8890gt, 12,299dwt, 144m, 8ha (4ho), 6x5tn cr, 14,960bhp Mitsui-B&W, 21.25kn. (*The Motor Ship*)

After delivery the *Canadian Reefer* (below) loaded cars at Emden for the US east coast, then sailed to Ecuador to load bananas for Basra. She demonstrated the class's versatility in 1981 with a record 11,000tn frozen citrus juice cargo in drums from Santos for Venezuela and the USA, and in 1982 on JL's New Zealand to Korea-Japan liner service with a cargo of 1238tn of frozen meat, 1364tn of frozen squid, 1080tn of squash, and 12 containers of onions below deck, and 70 containers of onions and 13 horses in boxes on deck. The squid was loaded at sea from Korean fishing vessels, for which exercise the *Canadian Reefer* had to be registered as a fish carrier to operate in New Zealand's exclusive economic zone. Fuel consumption of these ships was 69tn a day.

Canadian Reefer -- J Lauritzen A/S, Denmark; Aalborg Vaerft, Aalborg, 1979; 8849gt, 12,570dwt, 144m, 8ha (4ho), 6x5tn cr, 14,996bhp Helsingor-B&W, 22kn. (Tolerton)

Sevillan Reefer -- Scout Shipping Co (J Lauritzen), Liberia; Cia Euskalduna, Bilbao, 1967; 4366gt, 5300dwt, 134m, 4ha, 8x5tn der, 9600bhp Sulzer, 20kn. (Tolerton)

Iberian Reefer -- Scout Shipping Co (J Lauritzen), Liberia; Cia Euskalduna, Bilbao, 1968; 4366gt, 5123dwt, 134m, 4ha, 8x5tn der, 9600bhp Sulzer, 20kn. (Tolerton)

As well as the new buildings, Lauritzen augmented the fleet with pairs of secondhand purchases in the 1970s and 80s. The *Sevillan Reefer* and *Iberian Reefer*, completed in Bilbao in 1967 and 1968 respectively for local owner Naviera Vizcaina SA as the *Portugalete* and *Plencia*, were handsome reefers similar to many German-built reefers of the 60s and acquired in 1972. They were sold to Comninos Brothers in 1979.

Seen under later ownership (below) as the *Tajin*, the Drammen-built *Brazilian Reefer* and her sister *Belgian Reefer* from Howaldtswerke were bought from Bremen owner Scipio & Co in 1981. Completed in 1975 and 1974 respectively as the *Bremerhaven* and *Blumenthal*, they were among the fastest reefers ever built with a service speed originally of 23kn. They were owned by JL's Nassau subsidiary Frigg Shipping, but their fairly extravagant fuel consumption prompted their sale within five years. The *Tajin* as yard No.80 interrupted a long sequence of the Drammen standard reefers.

Tajin -- Liblease Four Ltd, St Vincent; Drammen Slip & Verk, Drammen, 1975; 5885/8423gt, 11,300dwt, 143m, 4ha, 8x5tn der, 23,400bhp 2xBlohm & Voss-Pielstick, 21kn. (Kees Lous)

For decades Lauritzen's red hulls and funnels were a dominating presence at the refrigerated cargo quays in ports all around the world, as the photo (top) of the *Manila Tiger* (1983/7777gt), formerly the *Reefer Tiger*, and *Anne B* (1983/12,383gt) sharing a wharf shows. Major reefer operators like Lauritzen augmented their owned fleet with large numbers of chartered vessels. The Shin Kurushima-built *EW Kilimanjaro* (1988/4988gt), centre, was one of the smaller chartered reefers to sport JL's colours. One of the first of the engines-aft, pallet-friendly reefers to establish the efficiency of this type for Lauritzen was another chartered ship, the Kishimoto Zosen-built *Reefer Badger* (1983/4128gt), below, pictured loading frozen fish direct from a trawler at a New Zealand port. A maiden voyage carrying Taiwanese bananas from Kaohsiung to Moji and Kobe, Japan, set the pattern for her trading for several months.

Anne B -- **Plum Reefer SA, Panama; Hashihama Zosen, Tadotsu, 1983; 12,383gt, 14,786dwt, 144m, 4ha, 4x10tn cr, 9450bhp IHI-Sulzer, 18kn. (Tolerton)**

The era of the ultra large reefer began when the *Anne B* (above) entered service in 1983, the first of eight similar 12,300gt, 16 and 18kn, pallet-friendly, engines-aft ships from Hashihama and Hyundai. Highly efficient though they were, they resembled bulk carriers more than traditional reefers and certainly signaled that the era of the classic dashing reefer was over. The *Anne B* and *Betty B* (below) were put into the Lauritzen pool by Norwegian owner Finn Bugge, but in 1992 were taken over by JL as the *Belgian Reefer* and *Brazilian Reefer* respectively. The modest speed was a contrast to reefers of the past, but so was the economic Sulzer engine consuming only 28tn a day. Able to carry 152 TEUs on deck, they both had four 10tn cranes.

Betty B -- **Peach Reefer SA, Panama; Hashihama Zosen, Tadotsu, 1984; 12,383gt, 14,803dwt, 144m, 4ha, 4x10tn cr, 9450bhp IHI-Sulzer, 18kn. (Tolerton)**

African Reefer -- Hol-Reefer V Ltd (Armada (Greece) Co), Cayman Islands; Hyundai, Ulsan, 1985; 12,411gt, 14,572dwt, 144m, 4ho, 4x8tn cr, 9600bhp Hyundai-B&W, 18kn. (Tolerton)

The *African Reefer* of 1985 (above), pictured in the late 90s when she was Cayman Islands-flagged, was one of the four Hyundai completions in this series and had 8tn cranes and four starboard side doors. A later large reefer for Lauritzen pool service was the *Mexican Reefer* of 1994 (below) from Shin Kurushima, and pictured in LauritzenCool colours after JL took over its big Scandinavian rival Cool Carriers. She and sister *Uruguayan Reefer* were designed to carry 4900 standard fruit pallets and 40 FEUs, all with reefer plugs.

Mexican Reefer -- Yaoki Shipping SA (Fleet Management), Panama; Shin Kurushima, Akitsu, 1994; 10,203gt, 11,575dwt, 144m, 4ha, 1x36tn & 3x8tn cr, 12,596hp Mitsubishi, 19.9kn. (Tolerton)

Chilean Reefer -- **Lauritzen ShipOwner A/S (Lauritzen Reefers AS), Denmark; Kvaerner Kleven Ulsteinvik, Ulsteinvik, 1992; 7944gt, 11,095dwt, 140m, 4ha, 4x8tn cr, 16,213bhp MAN, 22.3kn. (Tolerton)**

The five "Emperor Penguins" all completed in 1992 starting with the *Lapponian Reefer* have had a few twists and turns in their histories. The *Chilean Reefer* (above) was built as the *Carelian Reefer*, owned by Hollming OY, under Gustaf Erikson technical management, and in the Lauritzen pool, and carried bananas from Santa Marta to Jeddah on her first voyage. She was renamed in 1997. The *Scandinavian Reefer* (below) was the only one of the quintet to be completed for Lauritzen, although all operated in the Lauritzen reefer pool. On her first voyage she carried bananas from Guatemala and Colombia to the Middle East. These ships could carry 204 TEUs and cargoes at temperatures from minus 29 through to plus 14deg C in eight refrigeration zones.

Scandinavian Reefer -- **Lauritzen ShipOwner A/S (Lauritzen Reefers AS), Denmark; Kvaerner Kleven Leirvik, Leirvik, 1992; 7944gt, 11,054dwt, 140m, 4ha, 4x8tn cr, 14,592bhp MAN, 21.9kn. (Tolerton)**

Peruvian Reefer -- **Lauritzen Reefers A/S, Denmark; Kvaerner Kleven Ulsteinvik, Ulsteinvik, 1992; 7944gt, 11,095dwt, 140m, 4ha, 4x8tn cr, 16,212bhp MAN, 22.3kn. (Tolerton)**

The *Peruvian Reefer* (above) was built as the *Savonian Reefer* for Hollming/Erikson, and carried a rather unusual reefer mix of grapes, pears, and garlic on her first voyage. She was renamed in 1997. The *Bothnian Reefer* (below) was the only one of the five never owned by Lauritzen. Built for a Kvaerner company, she was taken on a long-term charter. Along with three of her sisters, she was also chartered early in her career by Geest for the Windward Islands-Central America-Zeebrugge banana run. In 2003 she was renamed *Wellington Star*.

Bothnian Reefer -- **Bothnian Reefer Ltd, Swan Reefer ASA, Liberia; Kaldnes, Tonsberg, 1992; 7944gt, 11,103dwt, 140m; 4ha, 4x8tn cr, 16,212bhp MAN, 21.75kn. (Tolerton)**

Reefer shipping moved into a new generation with the arrival of Lauritzen's four 14,400gt Family class ships from Lauritzen's own Danyard. The *Ditlev Lauritzen*, named after JL's founder, was first in 1990 followed by the *Ivar Lauritzen* the same year and the *Knud Lauritzen* and *Jorgen Lauritzen* in 1991. The world's largest pure reefers, they were designed for a crew of only six, but in fact initially operated with nine -- master, first officer, second officer, chief engineer, second engineer, radio officer, cook/steward, and two GP ratings. The advanced ship control system was designed for one-man navigation and engineroom and cargo control from the bridge.

Costing US$50m, the *Ditlev Lauritzen* was a milestone ship. On delivery in September 1990 she sailed to Montevideo to load palletised citrus fruit for Rotterdam and Dover, then demonstrated her container carrying ability by loading 238 40ft containers in Wilmington, North Carolina. In April 1991 she loaded a world record cargo of apples and pears in Napier, New Zealand, for Antwerp -- 425,362 cartons. Lauritzen's confidence in its new breed of reefer was quickly vindicated by her sisters, too. The *Ivar Lauritzen* on completion sailed via Las Palmas and Panama to load Ecuadorian bananas for Cork, Antwerp, and Hamburg, and on her third voyage carried 6953 pallets of deciduous fruit from San Antonio Este to Hamburg, Malmo, and Drammen. Later in 1991 she carried a record 6773 pallets of citrus fruit from Durban and Port Elizabeth to Mediterranean ports then concluded at Pembroke, and the same year the *Knud Lauritzen* carried a record Danish feta cheese cargo of more than 12,600tn from Esbjerg to Bandar Khomeini. On her maiden voyage the last of the quartet, the *Jorgen Lauritzen* (below), carried 6577 pallets of apples, pears, and oranges from Cape Town to Antwerp and Sheerness. The *Ivar Lauritzen* chalked up another world record with 53,695 drums of orange juice concentrate (14,634tn) from Santos for Ghent in November 1991.

Jorgen Lauritzen -- **J Lauritzen A/S, Denmark; Danyard, Frederikshavn, 1991; 14,406gt, 16,950dwt, 164m, 5ha, 3x36tn & 2x8tn cr, 13,758bhp Kawasaki-B&W, 19kn. (Trevor Jones)**

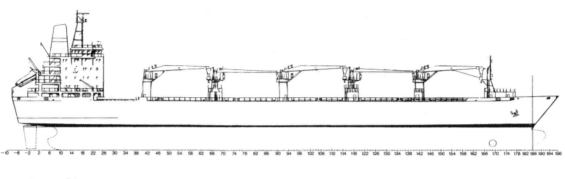

Ditlev Lauritzen -- **Sonderjysk Erhvervsinvestering K/S-17 (Lauritzen Reefers), Denmark; Danyard, Frederikshavn, 1990; 14,406gt, 16,950dwt, 164m, 5ha, 3x36tn & 2x8tn cr, 15,288bhp Korea HI-B&W, 20.2kn. (*The Motor Ship* and Kevin Moore)**

The first of the Lauritzen Family class reefers, the *Ditlev Lauritzen* of 1990.

CHAPTER NINE
SALENREDERIERNA

More than 20 years after the collapse of Sweden's Salen group, former Salen vessels still featured prominently in the world's reefer fleet. Salenrederierna was for many years the world's biggest reefer operator, and like its fellow Scandinavian giant J Lauritzen built ships whose individuality, class by class, made them instantly recognisable.

Unlike many of the Scandinavian shipping entrepreneurs with deep nautical roots, founder Sven Salen came from a farming family and started in rural journalism and banking before buying his first ships in 1915 when he was 25. The first appears to have been the 200tn motor barge *Robur*, but within a year or so he built up a fleet of seven small vessels, mainly sail. From 1922 Salen learned about both shipping and marketing bananas working for the Swedish Banana Co, importing bananas to Swedish and other Scandinavian ports with chartered ships, and eventually acquired this company. At the start of World War Two he had two ships plus three on order. Salen, an Olympic yachting bronze medalist in the six metre class at the 1936 games and inventor, it is said, of the genoa foresail, struck gold after the war developing his own reefer fleet.

His first reefer was the 3201gt *Sandhamn*, completed for Salen in 1941 by Oresundsvarvet, Landskrona, and Sweden's first refrigerated ship. Her first voyage was hardly a pointer to the success that was to come for the company in the reefer trades -- she docked in Gothenburg in May 1946 with a cargo of bananas from Panama that was already turning. The destruction of Germany's reefer fleet because of the war gave Salen an important contract to supply that country with bananas from Colombia and the impetus for the rapid growth of the Salen reefer fleet.

Salen also operated the passenger ship *Anna Salen* transporting refugees, and became a major tanker operator. Shortly before his death in 1969 Sven Salen christened his largest ship, the 210,000dwt tanker *Sea Sovereign*. The group's interests also encompassed dry bulk carriers, the Banana Co, oil rigs, air freight, retailing, real estate, and shipbuilding with Gotaverken.

However, it was the classes of handsome reefer ships that were to provide Salen's most enduring legacy, although the reefer fleet was largely the responsibility of Sture Odner from the 1950s until his retirement in 1982. Salen's blue funnel featured a white S with brackets above and below it, and, not surprisingly, Salen seafarers reckoned these represented the bananas which established the company's fortunes.

The company embarked on a refrigerated motorship construction programme in the 1950s with the 2054gt *Carlshamn* of 1951 from its own Ekensberg yard, followed by a series of 18kn ships all of around 6000gt -- the *Arawak* (1952), *Carib* (1953), *San Blas* (1955), and *Hispaniola* and *Cayman* (1956).

Salen opted for steam for the *Antigua* of 1960 and three 6900tn reefers (*Bolero*, *Barcarolle*, and *Ballade*) completed by La Ciotat in 1961-62, and all disposed of in 1972. More successful was the series of six A class 8000gt, 19kn ships from Eriksbergs -- the *Atitlan* and *Atlantide* of 1960, *Antilope*, *Ariel*, and *Argonaut* of 1964, and *Arawak* of 1965.

Salen returned to Eriksbergs for the *San Blas* and *San Bruno* (1967) and *San Benito* (1968), versatile 6414gt, 20kn ships suitable for both fruit and meat cargoes. A sister, the *Tasmanic* (1967), was also built by Eriksbergs for Rederi Transatlantic for Salen charter.

The eight-ship 22kn Snow class completed by La Ciotat in 1972-74 set a new standard for pure reefers -- 11,400gt, 173m overall, and with 22 compartments in five holds. These majestic ships were designed in consultation with United Brands, with which Salen had had a long and intimate trading association, and intended as versatile carriers for any reefer trade, with refrigeration down to minus 25deg C.

Devaluation of the franc during the building programme also made the vessels something of a bargain for Salen, and with their huge capacity of 17,319 cu/m the Snow class ships were very successful, particularly as fruit carriers. They had sidedoors port and starboard for all holds and banana conveyor hatches either side of the main crane houses for each hold, and also additional banana hatches inserted in the main hatches for holds 2, 3, and 4.

Interestingly, the wheel turned a full circle for four of the Snows -- in 2006 they were in the management of former Salen Reefer Services managing director Mats Ruhne's Holy House Shipping of Stockholm.

Another advance came with the six 11,700gt 22kn Winter class ships completed by Gotaverken in 1979-80. At 169m they were slightly shorter than the Snows but similar cargo carriers with a capacity of 17,100 cu/m. Of open hatch design the Winters, designed for palletised cargo, offered further handling efficiency, and unlike the Snows they had a significant container capability (240 TEUs). The bridge/accommodation was three-quarters aft, and the ships had four holds with twin hatches except for No.1 hold, and four sidedoors each side.

Using Salen's own multi-pallet loading system and four 16tn cranes, the Winters were designed to handle eight to 12 pallets a lift. New piggyback hatch covers for both the weather deck and tweendecks also assisted fast turnaround.

Salen claimed about one-third of the world reefer trade when the Winters went into service. Parent company Saleninvest filed for bankruptcy in December 1984 with reported debts of seven billion Swedish kroner. That year had also seen eight Spring class reefers from Japanese and South Korean yards put into service. Unlike previous designs for Salen, the 12,000grt Spring class had the engine right aft.

From the wreckage of Salen emerged Cool Carriers, with former Salen managers at the helm, and it quickly assumed Salen's mantle as the world's biggest reefer operator. Many of the Salen vessels found employment in Cool Carriers' livery, but two that didn't were the *Snow Hill* and *Snow Storm*, bought in 1985 as the *Noor* and *Hood* respectively by Irano-Hind Shipping Co of Tehran.

Snow class, from Chantiers Nav. de La Ciotat:
279 - 1972 *Snow Flower*, *Malayan Empress* 83, *Snow Flower* 85.
280 - 1972 *Snow Flake*, *South View* 84, *Blue Sea* 85, *Santos Star* 85, *Limari* 86, *Santos Star* 87, *Snow Delta* 96, *Santos Star* 00, to Chittagong for b/u 06.
281 - 1972 *Snow Land*, *Malayan King* 81, *South Fountain* 84, *Silver Tower* 85, *Chiquita Tower* 91, *Kyma* 94, *Snow Land* 97.
282 - 1972 *Snow Storm*, *Hood* 85, to Alang for b/u 00.

283 - 1973 *Snow Drift*, *South Cathay* 84, *Greenfield* 85, *Snow Drift* 89.
284 - 1973 *Snow Ball*, *Malayan Queen* 81, *South Joy* 84, *Gold Medal* 85, *Savona Star* 85, *Santiago Star* 88, *Snow Cape* 96, *Santiago Star* 00, to Chittagong for b/u 06.
285 - 1974 *Snow Hill*, *Noor* 85, to Alang for b/u 98.
286 - 1973 *Snow Crystal*, disabled by engineroom fire and towed to Durban 04.

Winter class
From Gotaverken Arendal:
913 - 1979 *Winter Moon*, *Zenit Moon* 85, *Winter Moon* 87, *Alcazar Carrier* 99.
914 - 1980 *Winter Sea*, *Zenit Sea* 85, *Winter Sea* 87, *Segovia Carrier* 99.
915 - 1979 *Winter Star*, *Zenit Star* 85, *Winter Star* 87, *Alicante Carrier* 99.
916 - 1979 *Winter Sun*, *Zenit Sun* 84, *Winter Sun* 87, *Algeciras Carrier* 00.
From Gotaverken Oresundsvarvet:
266 - 1979 *Winter Water*, *Zenit Water* 85, *Winter Water* 87, *Cadiz Carrier* 99.
267 - 1979 *Winter Wave*, *Zenit Wave* 85, *Winter Wave* 87, *Malaga Carrier* 99.

Spring class
From Koyo Dockyard, Mihara:
1055 - 1984 (launched as *Spring Blossom*), *Spring Ballad*, *Spring Panda* 85.
1056 - 1984 *Spring Blossom*, *Spring Bob* 85, considerable bottom damage from grounding off Kalundborg voyage Cuba-Baltic 89.
1057 - 1984 *Spring Bird*, *Spring Bee* 84, *Spring Bok* 02.
From Kurushima Dockyard, Onishi:
2283 - 1984 *Spring Breeze*, *Spring Tiger* 90.
2285 - 1984 *Spring Bride*, *Valencia Carrier* 02.
From Korea Shipbuilding & Engineering, Busan:
1022 - 1984 *Spring Delight*, *Spring Deli* 03.
1023 - 1984 *Spring Desire*, *Spring Dream* 89, abandoned after fire voyage Cape Town-Sheerness and towed to Cape Town seriously damaged 98, *Spring Dragon* 98, disabled with rudder problems near Panama Canal 00.
From Hyundai Heavy Industries, Ulsan:
271 - 1984 *Spring Dream*, *Spring Bear* 85.

Snow Drift at Durban (Kevin Moore)

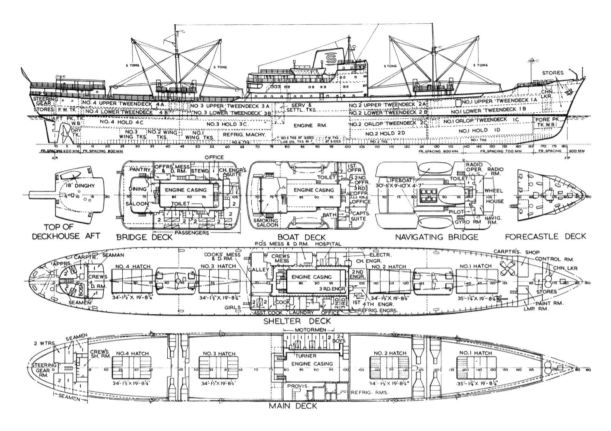

Atitlan -- **Salenrederierna A/B, Sweden; Eriksbergs, Gothenburg, 1960; 8067gt, 8433dwt, 148m, 4ha, 8x5tn der, 10,000bhp Eriksbergs-B&W, 18.5kn. (*The Motor Ship*)**

The 18.5kn *Atitlan* and *Atlantide* of 1960 from Eriksbergs were the first of a class of six reefers for Salen in the 1960s, and the state-of-the-art pair were said to be the largest banana carriers built so far. Of all-welded construction, they were also suitable for other refrigerated cargoes, with four holds with two continuous decks and two additional fruit decks in the forward holds and one in the after holds giving 14 cargo compartments.

The holds were insulated with fibreglass slabs with cork insulation on the decks and tanktops. The refrigeration machinery, with three main compressors, used freon 12 gas, and with indirect brine circulation in the air coolers in the cargo spaces different temperatures could be maintained for various different cargoes. Cargo handling was via eight 5tn derricks.

The ships could also carry 12 passengers, housed in six double-berth cabins on the bridge deck.

Altcar -- **Deanfield Co (Regal Marine Inc), UK; Eriksbergs, Gothenburg, 1965; 8020gt, 9042dwt, 149m, 4ha, 4x5tn cr, 10,000bhp Uddevallavarvet-B&W, 19kn. (Tolerton)**

The *Antilope*, *Ariel*, *Argonaut*, and *Arawak* had cranes instead of derricks. The last, *Arawak* of 1965 which had four 5tn cranes, was sold in 1978 to become the British-flag *Altcar*, named rather incongruously after a Lancashire village. She was managed by Piraeus company Regal Marine, but time-chartered back to Salen. She went to Taiwan breakers in 1984.

San Bruno -- **Rederi A/B Salenia (Salenrederierna), Sweden; Eriksbergs, Gothenburg, 1967; 6414gt, 8440dwt, 148m, 4ha, 4x5tn cr, 10,500bhp Eriksbergs-B&W, 20.25kn. (Trevor Jones)**

The *San Bruno*, pictured at Cape Town, and sisters *San Blas* (1967) and *San Benito* (1968) made up a handsome trio of reefers with bulbous bows and transom sterns for Salen from Eriksbergs, bridging the reefers of the 60s and the larger Snow and Winter classes to come. She had two tweendecks in the forward holds and one in the aft holds, the holds being insulated with fibreglass slabs coated with plastic.

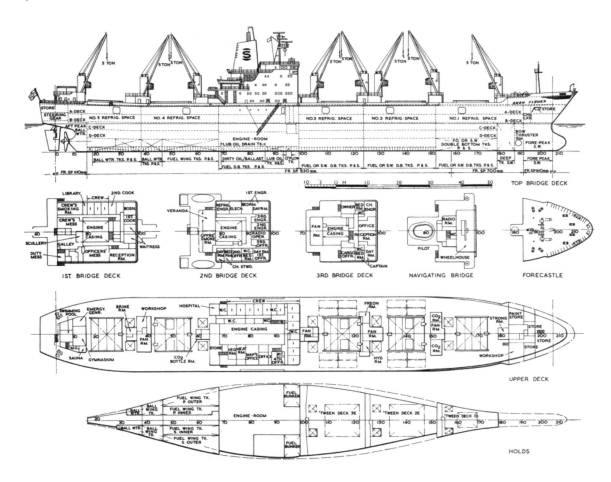

Snow Flower -- Salenrederierna A/B, Sweden; Ch Nav de La Ciotat, La Ciotat, 1972; 11,422gt, 12,782dwt, 173m, 5ha, 8x5tn cr, 23,202bhp Sulzer, 22.75kn. (*The Motor Ship*)

For some years the world's largest pure reefers (and too big for some services), the eight 22kn ships of the Snow class, built in 1972-74 in France for Salen, made up one of the great reefer ship classes. It appears four were still afloat in 2008. 'The Motor Ship' profile drawing (above) of the lead ship *Snow Flower* and the photograph of the *Snow Drift* of 1973 (below) in Universal Reefers colours illustrate their powerful, majestic lines.

Snow Drift -- Salenrederierna A/B, Sweden; Ch Nav de La Ciotat, La Ciotat, 1973; 11,406gt, 12,782dwt, 173m, 5ha, 8x5tn cr, 23,200bhp Sulzer, 22.75kn. (Kees Lous)

Santiago Star -- **Austasia Maritime Pte (Concordia Marine), Singapore; Ch Nav de La Ciotat, La Ciotat, 1973; 10,409gt, 12,782dwt, 173m, 5ha, 8x5tn cr, 23,200bhp CCM Sulzer, 22.75kn. (Tolerton)**

The *Snow Ball* of 1973 had frequent changes of name, becoming the *Malayan Queen* then *South Joy*, *Gold Medal*, *Savona Star* on Blue Star charter, and then, in 1988, the Nassau-registered *Santiago Star* (above). Pictured in Chilean owner Compania Sud Americana de Vapores' funnel colours, she became a "Snow" again eight years later as *Snow Cape* before reverting back to *Santiago Star*. In 1992 she and the *Santos Star* (ex-*Snow Flake*) had their holds rebuilt at Gdansk for carrying standard 2.1m high pallets. Both went to the breakers in 2006 when in spite of retaining their Blue Star names they were owned by Comninos' Target Marine. The *Snow Drift* of 1973 became the *South Cathay* and then the Hong Kong-registered *Greenfield* (below). The Snows were set up to carry a modest 16 containers on deck.

Greenfield -- **South Cathay Shipping (Wallem Shipmanagement), Hong Kong; Ch Nav de La Ciotat, La Ciotat, 1973; 10,705gt, 15,710dwt, 173m, 5ha, 8x5tn cr, 23,200bhp CCM Sulzer, 22kn. (Tolerton)**

Noor -- **Irano-Hind Shipping Co, Iran; Ch Nav de La Ciotat, La Ciotat, 1974; 14,363gt, 15,210dwt, 173m, 5ha, 8x5tn cr, 23,200bhp CCM Sulzer, 22kn. (Tolerton)**

The break up of Salen saw two of the class, the *Snow Hill* of 1974 and the *Snow Storm* of 1972, go to Iranian ownership with Irano-Hind Shipping Co as the *Noor* (above) and *Hood* (below) respectively. Registered in Bandar Abbas, they were the first Snows to go to the breakers, in 1998 and 2000 respectively, and both to Alang. Irano-Hind was a joint venture of Islamic Republic of Iran Shipping Lines (51%) and Shipping Corporation of India (49%).

Hood -- **Irano-Hind Shipping Co, Iran; Ch Nav de La Ciotat, La Ciotat, 1972; 14,379gt, 15,710dwt, 173m, 5ha, 8x5tn cr, 23,200bhp Sulzer, 22kn. (Tolerton)**

Winter Wave -- Salenrederierna A/B & Zenit Kylfinans A/B (Salen Reefer Services), Sweden; Gotaverken, Landskrona, 1979; 11,701gt, 15,100dwt, 169m, 7ha (4ho), 4x16tn cr, 20,500bhp Gotaverken-B&W, 22kn. (Trevor Jones)

The 22kn Winter class ships made up another series of imposing-looking reefers that in spite of Salen's tribulations were to give notable service. The *Winter Wave* is pictured in Swedish American funnel colours (above), and the *Winter Moon* (below) operating for Cool Carriers and flagged in Singapore after the demise of Salen. Both could carry 240 TEUs and had sidedoors port and starboard for every hold.

Winter Moon -- Hywellin Trading Pte, Singapore; Gotaverken, Gothenburg, 1979; 11,690gt, 15,200dwt, 168m, 7ha (4ho), 4x16tn cr, 20,500bhp Gotaverken-B&W, 22kn. (Trevor Jones)

The former Salen Snow class *Greenfield* (ex-*Snow Drift* of 1973) in Cool Carriers colours. The Salen bow crest, although painted over, is still clearly visible. (Tolerton)

Spring Delight **-- Partenreederei ms 'Spring Delight' (Ernst Jacob), Hong Kong; Korea SB, Busan, 1984; 12,783gt, 9891dwt, 152m, 7ha (4ho), 4x16tn cr, 10,400bhp Hyundai-B&W, 18kn. (Tolerton)**

Salen's Spring class vessels like the *Spring Delight* went into service for Cool Carriers. The *Spring Delight* had two sets of paired cranes, could carry 290 TEUs, and had sidedoors port and starboard for all four holds. She was also set up for vehicle carrying.

CHAPTER TEN

COOL CARRIERS

The collapse of Salen was followed forthwith by the creation of Cool Carriers, which in a relatively short time assumed its predecessor's mantle as the largest operator of reefer ships -- but with chartered rather than owned vessels.

Even before the collapse of Salen at the end of 1984, the directors of Salen Reefer Services had been planning to establish a new company should their parent run onto the rocks. SRS Reefers started operations the day Salen collapsed, backed by Swedish and US investors. The flagship Winter class ships were taken over by Swedish state-owned Zenit Shipping A/B after the collapse, swapping the "Winter" prefix for "Zenit" in the names of all six, before passing into Cool Carriers management.

In April 1985 the company was renamed Cool Carriers, and reestablished the Salen networks and contracts so successfully that within a few years it was the premier reefer operator. Within a couple of years a controlling interest in Cool Carriers was taken by Bilspedition AB, which also took over Transatlantic, Atlantic Container Line, and Gorthons.

Cool Carriers, with chartered ships tied to guaranteed minimum rates, was punished by a weak market in the early 90s and posted a US $14 million operating loss in 1993. In January 1994, Bilspedition sold a controlling interest to Avrista Ltd, an Isle of Man company 75 per cent owned by leading Norwegian shipowner Leif Hoegh, with the remaining stake purchased 21 months later.

Over 1994-1996 Hoegh through a Bermudan subsidiary spent US $172 million buying 10 modern, pallet-friendly reefers to strengthen the Cool Carriers fleet, and in 1996 joined with Safmarine to create Bermuda-registered Unicool, which with owned and chartered ships controlled more than 25 per cent of medium and large-size reefers.

At the end of 2000 Hoegh sold Cool Carriers to J Lauritzen for US $35.4 million, ending the great maritime rivalry between the Danish company and Cool Carriers and its predecessor Salen, and making the new LauritzenCool the world's largest specialist reefer operator. Taking effect from January 1, 2001, the transaction did not involve any vessel purchases. Cool Carriers president Mats Jansson was also named president of the new company.

Erikson Polar -- Temper Reefer Ltd (Rederiaktiebolaget Gustaf Erikson), Bahamas; Solisnor, Setubal, & Kleven, Leirvik, 1991; 5084gt, 5150dwt, 107m, 4ha, 4x6tn cr, 5496bhp Wartsila, 16kn. (Tolerton)

The distinctive appearance of the 5000gt, 16kn Erikson "Penguin" class is evident in these views of the *Erikson Polar* (above), renamed *Iberian Reefer* the year after her completion, and *Erikson Freezer* (below), which is now the *Green Freezer* and one of nine ships of this class in the very fast growing conventional fleet of Green Reefers of Norway.

Erikson Freezer -- Hol-Reefer II Ltd (Rederiaktiebolaget Gustaf Erikson), Bahamas; Kvaerner Kleven, Leirvik, 1991; 5084gt, 6120dwt, 109m, 4ha, 4x6tn cr, 5496bhp Wartsila, 16kn. (Tolerton)

CHAPTER ELEVEN

THE ERIKSON REEFERS

Prominent among the reefers of the 1990s are the twelve 5000gt, 16kn "Penguin" class sisters ordered for the famous Finnish company Gustaf Erikson. They may have been functional little ships, but there was a bit of nautical romance about them in the Erikson white and black funnel colours with its heritage going back to its founder's great barques of the last days of deepwater commercial sail.

Erikson contracted with J Lauritzen to operate and market the ships, the Danish company taking a shareholding in Erikson as part of the venture. Nassau-registered, the ships had four 6tn cranes serving their four holds, could carry 108 containers, and were conspicuous for their funnels offset to port, free-fall lifeboats, 360deg vision wheelhouses, and trunked hatches. Controllable pitch propellers and bow thrusters made them very manoeuvrable.

Norwegian builder Kvaerner Kleven subcontracted much of the work around yards in Finland, Portugal, and Norway. The first two, *Erikson Crystal* and *Erikson Arctic*, entered service three days apart in October 1989, and the pair both made their first loadings in South American ports for the USA. The next pair, *Erikson Cooler* and *Erikson Frost*, followed in March 1990.

In 1992 Kvaerner and Lauritzen announced the sale of the *Erikson Reefer* and *Erikson Polar* and a yet to be delivered ship by Kvaerner to Lauritzen, and the sale of the larger reefers *Anglian Reefer* and *Argentinean Reefer* to Kvaerner. The Penguin trio then took the traditional JL names *Indian Reefer*, *Iberian Reefer*, and *Italian Reefer* respectively. The *Erikson Cooler* had a tragedy early in her career, two engineers dying after being overcome by freon gas while making repairs on a Pacific voyage in 1991.

From Kleven, Ulsteinvik:
105 - 1989 *Erikson Crystal*, *Green Selje* 02.
109 - 1990 *Erikson Snow*, *Wisida Snow* 96, *Snow* 00, *Green Egersund* 01.
113 - 1991 *Erikson Nordic*, *Wisida Nordic* 96, *Nordice* 00, *Green Austevoll* 01.

From Kleven Loland, Leirvik:
106 - 1989 *Erikson Arctic*, *Belinda* 94, *Wisida Arctic* 96, *Arctic Ice* 00, *Green Karmoy* 01.
110 - 1990 *Erikson Winter*, *Wisida Winter* 96, *Wintertide* 00, *Green Maloy* 01.
114 - 1991 *Erikson Freezer*, *Green Freezer* 96.
The bow sections of the *Erikson Arctic* and *Erikson Winter* were built by Hasund, Ulsteinvik.

From Hollming, Rauma
275 - 1990 *Erikson Cooler*, *Green Cooler* 96.
276 - 1990 *Erikson Frost*, *Wisida Frost* 96, *Frost* 00, *Green Bodo* 01.
291 - 1992 *Italian Reefer*.
292 - 1992 *Carmencita*, *Green Crystal* 98.
The latter two vessels were completed at Leirvik and given the Kleven yard No's 115 and 116 respectively.

From Solisnor, Setubal:
142 - 1991 *Erikson Reefer*, *Indian Reefer* 92.
143 - 1991 *Erikson Polar*, *Iberian Reefer* 92.
The *Erikson Reefer* was completed at Ulsteinvik and the *Erikson Polar* at Leirvik with Kleven yard No's 111 and 112 respectively.

Erikson Frost -- **Wicoria Reefers Ltd (Rederiaktiebolaget Gustaf Erikson), Bahamas; Hollming, Rauma, 1990; 5084gt, 6120dwt, 109m, 4ha, 4x6tn cr, 5496bhp Wartsila, 16kn. (Tolerton)**

The *Erikson Frost* (top), one of four hulls built by Hollming, inaugurated a new service carrying meat from New Zealand to Los Angeles in 1991, intruding in what had been a container ship domain. The Penguins were regular visitors to New Zealand ports with Ecuadorian bananas in the '90s, frequently backloading beef to the US west coast. Less wanted for the *Frost* was a small literary claim to fame in "Serpent in Paradise," Dea Birkett's chronicle of life on Pitcairn -- and an amorous steward.

Detail of one of the Erikson ships (centre): The wheelhouse with its 360deg visibility, Erikson funnel, Lauritzen houseflag and crest -- and, not part of the corporate livery, a basketball hoop.

The *Erikson Snow* (below) was an all-Kleven completion. One of her first voyages was a cargo of potatoes from Egypt to Liverpool. Like the *Erikson Frost*, and most of her sisters she is now part of the Green fleet.

Erikson Snow -- **Wicoria Reefers III Ltd (Rederiaktiebolaget Gustaf Erikson), Bahamas; Kleven, Ulsteinvik, 1990; 5084gt, 6120dwt, 109m, 4ha, 4x6tn cr, 5496bhp Wartsila, 16kn. (Tolerton)**

Indian Reefer -- **Lauritzen Shipping (Bahamas) Ltd (Lauritzen Reefers AS), Denmark, 1991; Solisnor, Setubal, & Kleven, Ulsteinvik, 1991; 5084gt, 5150dwt, 109m, 4ha, 4x6tn cr, 5496bhp Wartsila, 16kn. (Tolerton)**

Two of the ships with Lauritzen "Reefer" names, the *Indian Reefer*, ex-*Erikson Reefer*, (above) with a Lauritzen funnel but still a white Erikson hull, and the *Italian Reefer* (below). The last Penguin completed, the *Italian Reefer* was the only one to enter service in the red JL livery, doing so when both JL's former ships of this name were still plying the seaways. She carried a familiar cargo for this class, bananas from Ecuador to New Zealand, on her first voyage. In 2007, still owned by Lauritzen, she was the only one of the 12 to have retained her original name.

Italian Reefer -- **Lauritzen Shipping (Bahamas) Ltd (J Lauritzen AS), Denmark; Hollming, Rauma, & Kleven, Leirvik, 1992; 5084gt, 6000dwt, 109m, 4ha, 4x6tn cr, 5495bhp Wartsila, 16kn. (Tolerton)**

The launch of the *Taupo* at Bartram's yard, Sunderland, in 1965. (APN)

CHAPTER TWELVE

THE P&O GROUP'S REEFERS

P&O constituents New Zealand Shipping Co and Federal Steam Navigation Co had nearly a century of experience in the New Zealand and Australian trades with cargo liners that were mixed general and refrigerated cargo carriers to draw on when they diversified into specialised reefers in their latter days as relatively autonymous companies within P&O.

The forerunner of these smaller, faster, dedicated reefers was NZSCo's *Turakina* of 1960, which also signaled a move away from their traditional runs. Built by Bartram & Sons at Sunderland, the 7707gt, 17kn *Turakina* was a single screw all-refrigerated ship apart from the forward portion of No.1 hold, and ordered along with Blue Star's *Canterbury Star* and Shaw Savill's *Amalric* for the developing Crusader Shipping Co New Zealand-Japan service.

NZSCo/Federal returned to Bartram for three in a series of four 8200gt reefers delivered in 1966-67 -- the *Taupo* and the *Tekoa* and *Tongariro* from Bartram, and the *Westmorland* from Lithgow, Glasgow. These 20kn ships were significantly faster than previous vessels in the fleet, and the first British ships fitted with Hallen derricks, which required only one winchman. Part of No.1 hold was non-insulated.

Both the *Tongariro* (on her maiden voyage) and then *Tekoa* set records for turnaround on the New Zealand coast loading for the UK, the latter loading 5287 tons in six and a half working days at Timaru in December 1967 using the port's new all-weather meat loaders. The record cargo comprised 4039 tons of lamb carcasses, 107 tons of mutton carcasses, 458 tons of cartoned sundries, 3663 bales of wool (including 2000 on deck), 101 tons of bulk tallow, 48 casks of casings, 192 sacks of seed, and 12 cases of general cargo. Her passage from Timaru to Belfast was 27 days at 18.98kn. These statistics lead to an interesting comparison on the changes in liner shipping in the latter part of the conventional cargo ship era. Exactly 10 years earlier NZSCo's previous *Tekoa*, a venerable 1922-built steamer, had loaded an almost identical tonnage starting at Auckland and finishing at Timaru, taking 14 and a half working days -- and then 42 days (at 12.46kn) on passage to the UK!

This quartet was followed in 1968 by the 9500gt, 21kn *Mataura* and *Manapouri*, which at a time of enormous change for the liner companies were built with an eye to wider trading than on just the traditional services. Price, delivery dates, and credit incentives led to the order going to Mitsui, Tamano, when contracts with a Japanese yard were still unusual for a traditional British company. They were renamed *Wild Mallard* and *Wild Marlin* and modified for reefer tramping in 1977 to operate for Lauritzen-Peninsular Reefers, and during this time and subsequent Greek ownership were to show their versatility in the tramp reefer trades.

"Wild" names had been first adopted earlier in the 70s when P&O/Federal formally diversified into tramp reefer trading with orders for two ships from Bergens, two from Lubecker, and four Drammen standards. The 7200gt, 22kn Bergens pair, sisters of the yard's "Super Core" ships for Maritime Fruit Carriers (see page 99), were delivered to Federal as the *Wild Auk* (1971) and

Wild Avocet (1972) and were followed by the *Wild Cormorant* and *Wild Curlew* -- vessels of very similar dimensions and speed but a quite different appearance -- from Lubecker in 1973.

In 1973-74 and 1977-78 four Drammen standard reefers also went into service for Federal/P&O (see Drammen Reefers, page 90).

Taupo class
From Bartram & Sons, Sunderland:
401 - 1966 *Taupo*, *Mandama* 80, to Chittagong for b/u 84.
402 - 1966 *Tekoa*, *Mahsuri* 80, to Kaohsiung for b/u 84.
403 - 1967 *Tongariro*, *Reefer Princess* 79, *Capetan Leonidas* 82, to Gadani Beach for b/u 85.
From Lithgows, Port Glasgow:
1158 - 1966 *Westmorland*, *Fares Reefer* 80, *Beacon Hill* 81, to Huangpu for b/u 85.

Mataura class
From Mitsui Zosen, Tamano:
786 - 1968 *Mataura*, *Wild Mallard* 77, *Macedonian Reefer* 81, *Maracaibo Reefer* 87, *Bolero Reefer* 88, *Corrado 1* 96, to Alang for b/u 98.
787 - 1968 *Manapouri*, *Wild Marlin* 77, *Marathon Reefer* 82, *Corfu Reefer* 87, *Limon Trader* 90, to Alang for b/u 99.

Bergens standard designs
From Bergens, Bergen:
651 - 1971 *Wild Auk*, *Olympian Reefer* 80, *Buenos Aires* 89, *Amazon Reefer* 95, to Mumbai for b/u 99.
653 - 1972 *Wild Avocet*, *Delphic Reefer* 80, *Aegean Reefer* 91, *Alpina I* 95, *Lima* 99, to Mumbai for b/u 99.

Wild Cormorant class
From Lubecker Flenderwerke, Lubeck:
602 - 1973 *Wild Cormorant*, *Attica Reefer* 81, *Silver Reefer* 85, *Bassro Nordic* 88, *Flamingo Reefer* 88, *Horncliff* 88, *Flamingo Reefer* 90, *Tuscan Star* 91, *Flamingo Reefer* 92, *Marathon Breeze* 96, to Alang for b/u 98.
603 - 1973 *Wild Curlew*, *Athenian Reefer* 81, *Golden Reefer* 85, *Bassro Arctic* 88, *Cariocas Reefer* 88, *Hornsea* 88, *Cariocas Reefer* 90, *Cap Corrientes* 90, *Cariocas Reefer* 92, to Mumbai for b/u 95.

Drammen standard designs
Wild Flamingo, *Wild Fulmar*, *Wild Gannet*, *Wild Grebe*. (see Drammen Reefers chapter)

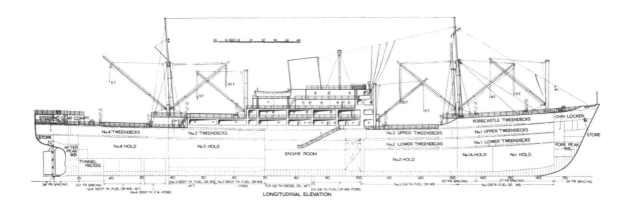

New Zealand Shipping Co's *Turakina* of 1960. (*The Motor Ship*)

Zaida -- British India SN Co, UK; Swan Hunter Shipbuilders, South Shields, 1972; 6088/8100gt, 132m, 4ho, 1x25tn cr, 12,000bhp Doxford, 18kn. (APN)

British India's funnel colours appeared, briefly and incongruously, on a reefer when the *Zaida* first entered service in 1972. Placed on the Crusader New Zealand-Japan run, she had provision for 50 containers on deck for the developing chilled beef trade to Japan, and two starboard side doors for unit loading. She and sister *Zira*, the last ships built for BI, were sold to Israel's Ofer Brothers in 1986.

147

Taupo -- **New Zealand Shipping Co, UK; Bartram & Sons, Sunderland, 1966; 8219gt, 11,866dwt, 160m, 5ha, 1x30 & 3x15 & 4x10tn der, 17,600bhp Clark-Sulzer, 19.5kn. (APN)**

Strikingly different in appearance from New Zealand Shipping Co's and Federal's traditional cargo liners were the quartet of reefers, each costing about two million pounds, delivered in 1966-67. As well as their more compact superstructures, bipod masts, and Hallen derricks, the *Taupo* (above), *Tekoa*, and *Tongariro* (below) from Bartram and *Westmorland* from Lithgow had light green hulls, with Federal funnels. The *Tongariro* was the last of the four.

Tongariro -- **New Zealand Shipping Co, UK; Bartram & Sons, Sunderland, 1967; 8233gt, 11,866dwt, 160m, 5ha, 1x30 & 3x15 & 4x10tn der, 17,600bhp Clark-Sulzer, 19.5kn. (APN)**

Tekoa -- Federal Steam Nav Co (P&O General Cargo Div), UK; Bartram & Sons, Sunderland, 1966; 8226gt, 11,325dwt, 160m, 5ha, 1x30 & 3x15 & 4x10tn der, 17,600bhp Clark-Sulzer, 19.5kn. (Tolerton)

The *Tekoa* (top) and *Taupo* (centre) in the P&O General Cargo Division livery, yellow (officially "corn") hull and blue funnel with white logo. Both were scrapped in 1984, the later after trading for four years as the Vestey group's Austasia Line's *Mandama* (bottom). Like so many British cargo liners of their era, their careers were lamentably short, and their sisters followed them to the breakers the next year.

Taupo -- Peninsular & Oriental Steam Nav. Co. (Tolerton)

Mandama -- Austasia Line, Singapore. (Tolerton)

The only Lithgow completion of the quartet, the *Westmorland* of 1966 was also the only one built for Federal, although all four spent part of their careers in Federal ownership during the shuffles of ownership and management within P&O in those days. At left is a view of the *Westmorland* during construction, with the aft end of No.2 hold and the upper and lower tween decks in the foreground, and the engine casing trunk visible between No.3 and 4 hatches. No.5 is covered by a tarpaulin during insulation work in the hold. She is illustrated below in a trials photo before her maiden voyage to Tasmania. Although launched 13 days after the *Taupo*, she pipped her sister into service.

Westmorland - **Federal Steam Nav Co, UK; Lithgows, Port Glasgow, 1966; 8230gt, 11,858dwt, 160m, 5ha, 1x30 & 3x15 & 4x10tn der, 17,600bhp Sulzer, 19.5kn. (both author's collection)**

Another view of the *Westmorland* in her original Federal livery (right). P&O sold her in 1980 to Raschid Fares, a Lebanese owner best known for operating livestock carriers, as the *Fares Reefer*, and in 1981 she was sold to the Blue Star-associated Dunston Shipping of Hong Kong as the *Beacon Hill* (below). Under this name she went to Chinese breakers in 1985. The distinctive funnel was red with a white band with black vertical stripes.

Beacon Hill -- **Dunston Shipping Co (Blue Star Ship Management), Hong Kong. She is pictured under the mechanical meat loaders at Timaru, New Zealand. (Tolerton)**

Macedonian Reefer -- Hampton Shipping Corp (Comninos Bros), Greece; Mitsui, Tamano, 1968; 9504gt, 11,919dwt, 164m, 7ha (5ho), 4x5tn cr, 3x25tn & 1x10tn der, 20,700bhp Mitsui-B&W, 20kn. (Tolerton)

Manapouri -- Federal Steam Nav Co, UK; Mitsui, Tamano, 1968; 9505gt, 11,705dwt, 164m, 7ha (5ho), 20,700bhp Mitsui-B&W, 21kn. (Tolerton)

Delphic Reefer -- Citragon Shipping Corp (Comninos Bros), Greece; Bergens, Bergen, 1972; 7291/9710gt, 10,963dwt, 155m, 5ha, 10x5tn der, 17,400bhp Akers-B&W, 22kn. (Tolerton)

The *Taupo* quartet was followed by the slightly larger Japanese-built *Mataura* and -- pictured centre in a rather rustic setting at Picton, New Zealand -- *Manapouri*. They had four holds forward and one aft, and were renamed *Wild Mallard* and *Wild Marlin* respectively in 1977. Greek owners Comninos Brothers, major reefer operators in the 1980s, were quick to snap up good quality vessels, and acquired both sisters, the *Mataura* as the *Macedonian Reefer* (above, chartered back for Lauritzen-Peninsular Reefers service). Comninos also bought the *Delphic Reefer* (bottom), formerly the *Wild Avocet* and one of two P&O reefers from Bergens.

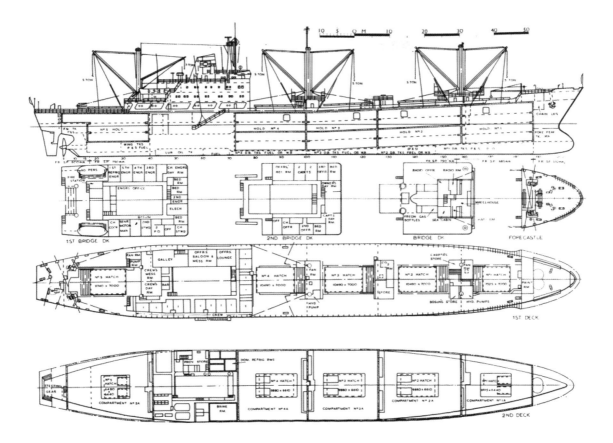

The *Wild Avocet*. (*The Motor Ship*)

Designed for worldwide trading, Federal's 21kn *Wild Avocet* of 1972 (above) and sister *Wild Auk* of 1971 from Bergens were part of a large series of similar ships from Aker group yards (see Maritime Fruit Carriers chapter). They went into the LPR pool.

The *Wild Curlew* (centre), pictured as built in Federal colours, and sister *Wild Cormorant* were products of Lubecker Flender-Werke. The yard later built the *Polar Costa Rica* and *Polar Honduras* for Hamburg-Sud to this design. Along with her sister, the *Wild Curlew* was yet another Comninos acquisition, becoming their *Athenian Reefer* (bottom) in 1981.

Wild Curlew -- Federal Steam Nav Co, UK; Lubecker Flender-Werke, Lubeck, 1973; 7594gt, 9169dwt, 154m, 4ha, 8x6tn der, 17,100bhp MAN, 22.5kn. (Tolerton)

Athenian Reefer -- Initial Shipping Services Corp (Comninos Bros), Greece. (Tolerton)

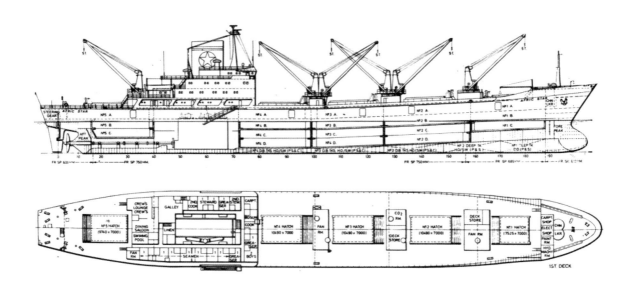

Blue Star's long involvement with conventional reefer ships culminated in the *Afric Star* class (above) and *Scottish Star* class (below). (*The Motor Ship*)

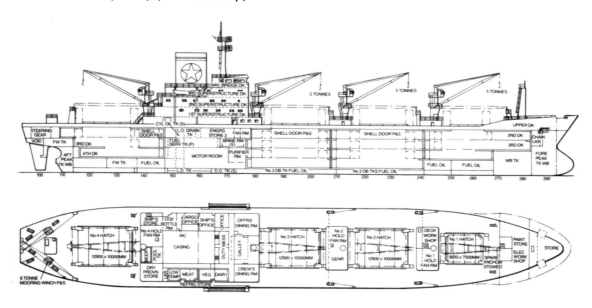

CHAPTER THIRTEEN

BLUE STAR AND
STAR REEFERS

Blue Star and the Vestey group's involvement in refrigerated shipping spanned many decades back to before World War One, but its commissioning of its six A class ships, pure reefers for tramp trading, in the mid-1970s marked a new venture.

The *Afric Star*, *Andalucia Star*, *Avelona Star*, *Almeda Star*, and *Almeria Star* from Smith's Dock, Middlesbrough, in 1975-76 and the *Avila Star* from Nakskov, Denmark, in 1975 were designed as versatile 24kn ships to carry cargoes ranging from frozen meat to dairy products and bananas and deciduous and citrus fruits. The hull design was essentially the same as the Norwegian Aker *Wild Auk* and *Wild Avocet* 9700gt reefer design for Federal Steam Navigation and similar ships for Maritime Fruit Carriers, and construction of the *Avila Star* was subcontracted by Aker to Nakskov. However, the Blue Star ships were fitted with six 5tn cranes instead of derricks -- and much more imposing funnels. All except the *Almeria Star* revived famous Blue Star names of the past.

Five holds, four forward of the machinery and one aft, provided 14,250 cu/m of refrigerated cargo space in 18 compartments, and the refrigeration plant permitted temperatures from plus 13 down to minus 25deg C.

The first cargo of the lead ship *Afric Star* was bananas from Esmeraldas and Guayaquil, Ecuador, and Turbo, Colombia, for Cork and Antwerp.

As well as operating on the usual reefer runs, the *Avelona Star* and *Andalucia Star* both saw service as floating supermarkets in the Falkland Islands in the wake of the 1982 war. The *Avelona Star* was chartered by the UK Ministry of Defence while unloading South African apples at Sheerness and carried some of this cargo back to the South Atlantic when she sailed for the Falklands when the war was still under way. During two years on Falklands duty she made five voyages to the islands and spent long weeks anchored as a storage ship. The *Andalucia Star* made three voyages.

Apart from the *Avila Star* which had been sold to Norwegian owners in 1979 as the *Hidlefjord* and chartered back, the As were nominally sold to the ownership of one-ship Hong Kong companies under Wallem management in the 1980s, and chartered back to Blue Star. Four went in 1984 and the *Afric Star* in 1987. Except for the *Andalucia Star*, which found a new career as a fruit juice carrier, they came back into the Blue Star fold in 1988 under their original names. That same year the A class were modified to meet the industry standard of 2.2m deck height for carrying pallets.

In 1983 Blue Star placed a 70 million pounds order with Harland & Wolff, Belfast -- the birthplace of many previous ships for the company, notably the famous series of "Empire Food Ships" commencing with the *Imperial Star* of 1934 -- for four 10,500gt ships. Designed to handle both refrigerated and general cargoes and both pallets and containers (106 TEUs), these ships, the ultimate British conventional reefers, have, like the A class, proved very successful.

A fire aboard the lead ship *English Star* during the latter stages of fitting out gave the *Scottish Star* the distinction of being the first to be delivered in 1985, followed by the *Auckland Star* the same year and the *English Star* and *Canterbury Star* in 1986.

The 11,200kW Harland & Wolff-B&W seven cylinder engines made the class considerably more fuel efficient than comparable ships of just a few years earlier, consuming 27tns a day at 18kn. They had a maximum service speed of nearly 20kn and were designed for a crew of 21, compared with the 36 of the A class.

Four holds, three forward of the machinery and one aft, gave 13,172 cu/m capacity, and each was served by a 5tn electric crane. No.2 and 3 holds had four decks and 1 and 4 had three. The full range of refrigerated cargoes could be carried at eight different temperatures. All 14 compartments had a clear deck height of 2.2m for container and pallet stowage, and the extremes of holds 1 and 4 had movable panels to square off the cargo space.

MacGregor-Navire insulated folding hydraulic steel hatch covers were fitted for the weather and tween deck hatches, with banana openings, and MacGregor side doors were fitted at upper tween deck level for each hold.

The refrigeration system used three screw compressors with R22 as the primary refrigerant, with separate air coolers and vertical upwards air circulation for each of the 14 compartments, designed for 90 air circulations an hour and forced air refreshing to give three changes an hour.

The early voyages of the *Scottish Star* were in the fruit trades. She sailed from Belfast in ballast in April 1985, to load boxed bananas at Santo Tomas, Guatemala, and Turbo, Colombia, for Marseilles and Savona, then loaded palletised tomatoes, aubergines, and potatoes in Tenerife and Las Palmas, Canary Islands, for discharge at Newhaven. The *Scottish Star* then carried 95 empty containers loaded at Newhaven and Le Havre to New Zealand to position for a palletised kiwifruit cargo, loaded in Tauranga and Nelson, for Zeebrugge and Bremen, before loading a second kiwifruit cargo of 4863 pallets (about 32 million individual fruits) at Gisborne and Tauranga for Zeebrugge.

Her first visit to South Africa came early in 1986 to load a full cargo of deciduous fruit at Cape Town.

On one of her early voyages the *English Star* made the first Blue Star call in Ireland for more than 10 years, loading frozen beef in Dublin for Santos, Brazil, in 1986.

Before the *Scottish Star* quartet entered service, Blue Star had made an addition to its conventional reefer fleet by chartering four new Japanese-built and owned reefers for five years, with a purchase option. The 10,500gt *Atlantic Star* and *Pacific Star* and similar 9600gt *Baltic Star* and *Tasman Star* were launched with Blue Star names at Sasebo in 1983.

Four-hold vessels of a similar configuration to the *Scottish Star* class but with five cranes, they were particularly suitable for fruit carrying and also suitable for vehicle carrying. Six months after entering service in November 1983, the *Baltic Star* became the first conventional reefer to carry a full export cargo of New Zealand kiwifruit, loading pallets in Nelson and Tauranga for Zeebrugge. The kiwifruit trade was growing fast at this time, and the NZ Kiwifruit Authority estimated the costs were 45 per cent lower than shipping by container.

In 1988 Blue Star and Hamburg-Sud announced they would combine their reefer fleets in a joint venture run from London from January 1 1989 under the new title Star Reefers, initially with about 25 mainly modern pallet-friendly ships. When Blue Star disposed of its container shipping interests to P&O Nedlloyd in 1998, Vestey's tramp reefer component was renamed Albion Reefers, while maintaining the Star Reefers operation with Hamburg-Sud.

The Vestey involvement ended when Star Reefers/Albion Reefers was sold for US$34.8m in 2001 to Cayman Islands-based, Siem Industries-owned Swan Reefer, a listed Oslo company -- Swan adopting the better-known Star Reefers title. Swan Reefer had expanded quickly in the 1990s through mergers and acquisitions in Norway which brought together firstly Oslo operator Irgens Larsen, whose owner Harry Irgens Larsen had died in 1982, then Kvearner Shipping and Swan Shipping, with the Swan Reefer name then being adopted. Swan took over six owned ships (*Auckland Star*, *Canterbury Star*, *English Star*, *Scottish Star*, *Trojan Star*, and *Tudor Star*) and 18 chartered ships from Vestey in the 2001 acquisition.

On the heels of Star Reefers acquisition by Swan, the new owners quickly created a short-lived joint operation with Japan's NYK to create NYK Star Reefers, which ranked as the second-largest reefer operator after LauritzenCool. This pool was dissolved by mutual agreement two years later at the end of 2003.

A class, from Smith's Dock, Middlesbrough:
1328 - 1975 *Afric Star*, *Lanark* 87, *Afric Star* 88, arrived Alang 01 for b/u.
1329 - 1975 *Andalucia Star*, *Fife* 84, *Orange Star* 86 (converted to fruit juice tanker 87).
1330 - 1975 *Avelona Star*, *Castle Peak* 84, *Avelona Star* 88, *Hornsound* 90, *Avelona Star* 90, aground off Terneuzen undamaged 90, *Baltic Wind* 01.
1331 - 1976 *Almeda Star*, *Arran* 84, *Harlech* 84, *Almeda Star* 88, *Baltic Wave* 01.
1332 - 1976 *Almeria Star*, *Perth* 84, *Almeria Star* 88, *Avila Star* 90, *Ice Bell* 03,

A class, from Nakskov Skibsvaerft:
208 - 1975 *Avila Star*, *Hidlefjord* 79, *Swan Lake* 88, *Hornstream* 92, *Sun Swan* 92, *Reefer Sun* 93.

Scottish Star class, from Harland & Wolff Shipbuilding, Belfast:
1722 - 1985 *Scottish Star*.
1723 - 1985 *Auckland Star*, *Horncliff* 87, *Auckland Star* 89.
1721 - 1986 *English Star*, *Hornsea* 87, *English Star* 89.
1724 - 1986 *Canterbury Star*.

Baltic Star class, from Sasebo Heavy Industries, Sasebo:
322 - 1983 *Baltic Star*, *Baltic Start* 02.
323 - 1983 *Tasman Star*, *Tasman Start* 01.
324 - 1983 *Atlantic Star*, *Atlantic Start* 01, seriously damaged by fire Izola shipyard 01, *Stina* 03.
325 - 1984 *Pacific Star*, *Pacific Start* 02, *Amalia* 02.

Townsville Star **-- Salient Shipping Co (Bermuda), UK; Bremer Vulkan, Vegesack, 1957; 8230/10,632gt, 12,353dwt, 157m, 5ha, 1x50, 1x15, 2x10, 9x5, 8x3tn der, 11,250bhp Bremer Vulkan-MAN, 17kn. (Tolerton)**

Forerunners of the successful A class tramp reefers of the 70s were a number of ships built for Blue Star in the late 50s-early 60s as new trades evolved.

The sisters *Gladstone Star* and *Townsville Star* (above), both delivered in 1957, were among five ships rather controversially ordered from Germany (Bremer Vulkan) in the 1950s. Both were built for the Blue Star subsidiary Salient Shipping Co of Bermuda, but reregistered in London in 1958. Still looking spick and span, the *Townsville Star* is pictured in 1980 shortly before her sale that year to breakers in Taiwan.

Very similar to these ships both in size and for their array of cargo gear including a 50tn derrick were the *Rockhampton Star* of 1958 (opposite, top) and sister *Queensland Star* of 1957, from Cammell Laird and Fairfield respectively. Designed for a new service direct from Queensland ports to the UK via Torres Strait, they had compartments for chilled beef as well as the freezer spaces. The *Rockhampton Star* was sold in 1981 to become the *Golden Lady* and went to the breakers at Chittagong two years later.

Notable when she was built for her array of nine cranes -- unique on a British ship at that time -- and hydraulically-operated hatch covers, the *Fremantle Star* of 1960 (opposite, bottom) was another Cammell Laird completion. She went to Kaohsiung breakers at the end of 1979.

Rockhampton Star -- Blue Star Line, UK; Cammell Laird, Birkenhead, 1958; 7474/9847gt, 12,062dwt, 154m, 5ha, 1x50 2x15 4x10 6x5 8x3tn der, 13,300bhp Harland & Wolff-B&W, 17kn. (Tolerton)

Fremantle Star -- Blue Star Line, UK; Cammell Laird, Birkenhead, 1960; 8403gt, 12,120dwt, 158m, 5ha, 5x5 & 4x3tn cr, 2x15 & 2x10tn der, 13,300bhp H&W-B&W, 18kn. (Tolerton)

159

Avelona Star -- **Avelona Star Ltd (Blue Star Ship Management), UK; Smith's Dock, South Bank, Middlesbrough, 1975; 7618/9784gt, 11,092dwt, 155m, 5ha, 6x5tn cr, 17,400bhp Kincaid-B&W, 24kn. (Tolerton, top, and Trevor Jones, lower)**

The six fast A class were successful ships which had long careers. Fourth of the class was the *Avelona Star*, pictured in a New Zealand port loading meat for the USSR (top) and at Cape Town (lower). This ship was taken up by the UK Ministry of Defence in May 1982 during the Falklands war for service as a stores ship, and, as can be seen in the first photo, had a stern helipad fitted at Portsmouth, as well as replenishment at sea equipment, a freshwater generating plant, garages, and extra accommodation. Working at Port Stanley or San Carlos, the *Avelona Star* dispatched 353 loads by helicopter and 1498 by alongside transfer during more than three months at the Falklands on her first assignment there.

Andalucia Star -- Blue Star Line (Blue Star Ship Management), UK; Smith's Dock, Middlesbrough, 1975; 7618/9784gt, 11,092dwt, 155m, 5ha, 6x5tn cr, 17,400bhp Kincaid-B&W, 24kn. (Tolerton)

Three more A class -- the *Andalucia Star* (top), *Almeria Star* (centre), and *Almeda Star* (below). Like the *Avelona Star*, the *Andalucia Star* made Falklands voyages on charter to the UK MoD. In 1986 she was converted to a fruit juice carrier, the *Orange Star*. Uniquely among the six As, the *Almeria Star* operated with two different Blue Star names, being renamed the *Avila Star* in 1990.

Almeria Star -- Transport Exchange Co (Blue Star Ship Management), UK; Smith's Dock, Middlesbrough, 1976; 7615/9781gt, 11,093dwt, 155m, 5ha, 6x5tn cr, 17,400bhp Harland & Wolff-B&W, 24kn. (Tolerton)

Almeda Star -- Avelona Star Ltd (Blue Star Ship Management), UK; Smith's Dock, Middlesbrough, 1976; 7615/9781gt, 11,092dwt, 155m, 5ha, 6x5tn cr, 17,400bhp Harland & Wolff-B&W, 24kn. (Tolerton)

Harlech -- **Arran Shipping Ltd (Wallem Shipmanagement), Hong Kong. (Tolerton)**

Five of the six A's were nominally sold during the 1980s to one-ship Hong Kong companies managed by Wallem, but chartered back to Blue Star and still had a Blue Star look about them, as these photographs of the *Harlech* (above), ex-*Almeda Star*, and *Fife* (below), ex-*Andalucia Star*, show. At left and right are the funnels of the *Harlech* and *Fife* -- both painted in the traditional Blue Star orange/red.

Fife -- **Highvale Ltd (Wallem Shipmanagement), Hong Kong. (Tolerton)**

Hidlefjord -- S/A Hidlefjord & S/A Byfjord (Kornelius Olsen), Norway; Nakskov Skibsvaerft, 1975; 7600/9766gt, 11,093dwt, 155m, 5ha, 6x5tn cr, 17,400bhp Nylands-B&W, 24kn. (Tolerton)

The curiosity among the A class was the *Avila Star* of 1975 which was built by the Danish Nakskov shipyard, and after four years sold to Stavanger owner Kornelius Olsen as the *Hidlefjord* for, as the photo shows, charter back to Blue Star.

Atlantic Star -- Taihei Shosen KK, Japan; Sasebo HI, Sasebo, 1983; 10,535gt, 10,601dwt, 151m, 4ha, 5x10tn cr, 14,400bhp Mitsubishi, 19.5kn. (Tolerton)

Bridging the A class and *Scottish Star* class were four Japanese ships built for charter to Blue Star like the *Atlantic Star* of 1983. All four were completed at Sasebo in 1983-84. They had four sidedoors port and starboard and fuel consumption of the *Atlantic Star* was 33tn a day.

Scottish Star -- **Lombard Leasing Metropolitan Ltd (Blue Star Ship Management), Bahamas; Harland & Wolff, Belfast, 1985; 10, 291gt, 13,058dwt; 150m, 4ha, 4x5tn cr, 15,226bhp Harland & Wolff-B&W, 19kn. (Kees Lous)**

A fire on the lead ship *English Star* during fitting out meant the *Scottish Star* (above) was the first into service of Blue Star's new 10,500gt class from Harland & Wolff, followed by the *Auckland Star* (below). Like the A class ships, these four ships, delivered in 1985-86, were very handsome modern reefers. Both are illustrated on charter to Fyffes with that company's buff funnel with black top.

Auckland Star -- **Investors in Industry PLC (Blue Star Ship Management), Bahamas; Harland & Wolff, Belfast, 1985; 10,691gt, 11,434dwt, 150m, 4ha, 4x5tn cr, 15,226bhp H&W-B&W, 19.5kn. (David Salisbury/collection Trevor Jones)**

Canterbury Star -- 3i plc (Blue Star Ship Management), Bahamas; Harland & Wolff, Belfast, 1986; 10,291gt, 11,434dwt, 150m, 4ha, 4x5tn cr, 15,226bhp Harland & Wolff-B&W, 20kn. (Trevor Jones, above, & Kevin Moore, below)

Two views of the *Canterbury Star* at Durban, in traditional Blue Star livery (above) and in the later and rather less distinguished Star Reefers colours (below). The funnel is white with red top over a narrow blue band, and blue star outlined in red. Originally British-flagged, the quartet was later registered in Nassau.

Norman Star -- **Estelargo Maritime Co (Dobson Fleet Management), St Vincent & the Grenadines; Koyo Dockyard, Mihara, 1979; 10,153gt, 9996dwt, 168m, 4ha, 10x5tn & 2x3tn der, 14,400bhp IHI-Sulzer, 21kn. (Tolerton)**

A Blue Star funnel and a traditional Blue Star name -- but with a variety of previous names and flying the flag of St Vincent, the 1979-built *Norman Star* was perhaps an incongruous addition to the fleet. She had had traded as the *Humboldt Rex*, *Humboldt Rex No.2*, and *EW Andes* before the famous Blue Star funnel was painted up on her in 1994, along with her sister *Saxon Star*, ex-*Tasman Rex*.

Avila Star -- **Star Reefers Shipowning Inc (Fleet Management), Bahamas; AESA, Puerto Real, 1990; 11,590gt, 12,519dwt, 158m, 4ha, 4x19tn cr, 11,800hp AESA-B&W, 18.5kn. (Kevin Moore)**

Another secondhand addition in the 1990s was the *Avila Star*, one of the series of nine similar reefers from Astilleros Espanoles. Built as the *Del Monte Trader*, she became the *Tundra Trader* in 1999 and *Avila Star* in 2004. Designed for pallet carriage like most reefers of her generation, she can also carry up to 362 TEUs, including 290 refrigerated.

Caribbean Star -- **Star Reefers Shipowning (Fleet Management), Panama; Shikoku Dockyard, Takamatsu, 1997; 11,435gt, 10,362dwt, 154m, 4ha, 2x36tn & 2x8tn cr, 15,599hp Mitsui-B&W, 20.3kn. (Kees Lous)**

The introduction of a quartet which included the *Caribbean Star* (above) and *Cote d'Ivoirian Star* (below), both from Shikoku Dockyard, brought some non-traditional Blue Star names into the Star Reefers fleet. Both are specially suitable for vehicle carrying and have container capacities of 254 and 374 TEUs respectively, and fuel consumption of about 51tn a day. The former also traded as the *Hornsea* from 1998 to 2000. What's a modern reefer worth? Two of the quartet, the *Caribbean Star* and *Costa Rican Star*, jointly cost US$39.8m when Star Reefers bought them outright in 2003. In contrast the *Townsville Star* which started this chapter cost 1.25 million pounds.

Cote d'Ivoirian Star -- **Green Spanker Shipping SA (Kyowa Kisen), Panama; Shikoku Dockyard, Takamatsu, 1998; 11,733gt, 10,350dw, 154m, 4ha, 2x36tn & 2x8tn cr, 16,680hp Mitsui-B&W, 21kn. (Kees Lous)**

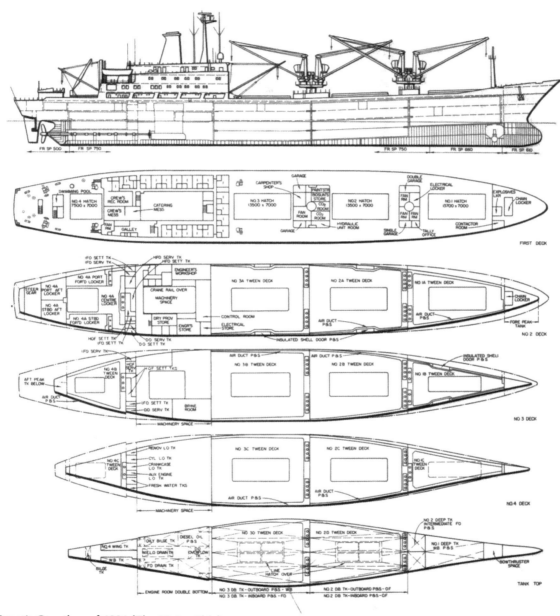

Geest's *Geestbay* of 1981 (*The Motor Ship*)

CHAPTER FOURTEEN

GEEST LINE

The Geest Line is synonymous with a long series of handsome ships distinguished by twin exhaust uptakes instead of a conventional funnel, but the company's first excursion into this sphere of shipping was even more radical.

Brothers John and Leonard van Geest came from the Netherlands to Spalding, Lincolnshire, in 1936 to extend the van Geest family's business interests by importing produce and bulbs from home, and Geest became one of the UK's largest privately-owned firms with diverse fruit distribution, horticulture, light engineering, shipping, and other interests. Geest acquired its first ship in 1946 to carry produce from the Netherlands. Looking for a year-round commodity to anchor its operations, Geest took the huge gamble in 1952 of challenging the Fyffes/Jamaica Producers monopoly of the West Indies-UK banana trade by contracting to take the entire crop of the Windward Islands. Geest sustained the trade with chartered ships until the 1900gt Dutch-flag *Geestland* and *Geeststar* entered service in 1960.

Built by C Amels & Zoon, Makkum, and De Groot & van Vliet, Slikkerveer, respectively, the pair had machinery and bridge aft, and a bulbous bow. Even more unconventionally, they were gas turbine-powered (the first such ships built in the Netherlands), with four Werkspoor free-piston gasifiers supplying gas to a 4000shp Brown Boveri turbine. *Geestland* also had the distinction of being the first oceangoing ship with teleprinter communications. The ships had two holds with upper and lower tweendecks, and a speed of 17.6kn. Like a number of other experiments with gas turbine propulsion, the results did not apparently meet expectations, and the pair were later converted to motorships.

The familiar Geest profile with two slender funnels abreast was introduced with the company's next ships, the British-flagged 7891gt *Geestbay* and *Geestport* of 1964 from Netherlands Dock, Amsterdam. Geest carried a record 14,290,680 stems from the Windward Islands in 1965, and the next year introduced two similar ships to the 1964 pair, the *Geestcape* and *Geesthaven* from Scott's Shipbuilding, Greenock.

These ships could carry 200,000 stems of bananas in five holds, and carried general cargo outwards. The quartet, like the Geest ships to follow them, also carried 12 passengers on what became a very popular run for sea travelers.

Geest's policy of disposing of vessels after eight to 10 years saw the company return to Scott's for four more ships, commencing with the three-hold, 5871gt, 21kn *Geest-tide* of 1971 and followed by the *Geestcrest* and *Geestland* in 1972 and *Geeststar* in 1973. The *Geest-tide* also introduced provision for 340 containers.

Geest's series of distinctive ships reached its apogee with a 25 million pounds contract for the 19.6kn, 7729gt *Geestbay* of 1981 and *Geestport* of 1982, both from Smith's Dock, Middlesbrough.

This pair had four holds, three hatches forward of the superstructure and one aft, and 12,900cu/m of cargo space. Again set up for 12 passengers, the pair had a crew of 40.

The hull shape was similar to the Blue Star A class built at Smith's a few years earlier, but a little broader aft to suit a shallower draught. The *Geestbay* reflected evolution in this trade with all the holds except No.1 designed for pallets, five cargo lockers in No.4 upper tweendecks for exotic fruit, and provision for 72 TEUs (20 on deck and 52 in the holds).

The refrigeration plant -- three 240kW single-screw compressors serving the holds (and a smaller 75kW compressor for the No.4 hold lockers) -- was designed to cool a full cargo of bananas from a loading temperature of 28deg C to a carriage temperature of 12deg C in 36 hours, and cargo could be frozen to minus 20deg C.

The classic *Geest* profile -- and the passenger service -- disappeared when the company sold the *Geestport* and *Geestbay* in 1994 as the *Bahiana Reefer* and *Magellan Reefer* respectively.

By then Geest had introduced the more prosaic 20.3kn, 13,077gt *Geest St. Lucia* and *Geest Dominica*, both 1993 completions from Danyard, Frederikshavn and registered in the Bahamas, to the run. Their overall length of 158m was almost identical to the 1981-82 pair, but with engines and bridge aft the two new five-hold ships had a much greater capacity of 16,990 cu/m. They could also carry 439 TEUs. The cargo gear was all cranes -- two 20tn and two 8/36tn.

When Geest started the Windward Islands service, it had been an impertinent challenge to Fyffes' hegemony in the banana trade to Britain. But Fyffes had the last laugh -- in December 1995 a consortium of Fyffes and the Windward growers took over Geest's banana importing business.

The lines of a former Geest ship are unmistakable -- the *Geestcrest* of 1972 in later guise as the Soviet *Kandava*. (Tolerton)

Geestland -- **Waling van Geest & Sons, Netherlands; C Amels & Zoon, Makkum, 1960; 1937gt, 2119dwt, 100m, 2ha, 2x3tn der, 4 Werkspoor free piston gasifiers & 1 Brown Boveri gas turbine, 17kn. (World Ship Society)**

The innovative Dutch-built *Geestland* of 1960, the company's first owned ship, had gas turbine propulsion, and with her machinery aft had a rather modern profile for a reefer designed in the 1950s. Later converted to a motorship, she was sold in 1971 to Panamanian owners as the *Banana Planter*. The large deckhouse forward of the bridge was for meat cargoes outwards, and used for additional banana space on the returns.

Geestbay -- **Geest Industries, UK; Nederland Dok, Amsterdam, 1964; 7891gt, 8010dwt, 148m, 3ha (5ho), 2x10 & 8x5tn der, 10,500bhp Sulzer, 21kn. (World Ship Society)**

The characteristic twin funnel Geest profile was introduced to the fleet with the Dutch-built *Geestbay* and her sister *Geestport*, both 1964 British flag completions from Nederland Dok. She was sold to Norwegian owners as the *North Star* after only nine years. Frequent upgrading was the pattern for Geest.

Geeststar -- **Geest Industries, UK; Scott's Shipbuilding, Greenock, 1973; 5871gt, 7654dwt, 149m, 3ha, 3x8tn cr, 6x5tn der, 12,000bhp Scott's-Sulzer, 21kn. (World Ship Society)**

Geest received four more ships in the early 70s, all from Scott's, culminating in the *Geeststar* (above) of 1973. She is pictured (below) after being sold to a Laskaridis company in 1986 to become the Cypriot *Frio Brazil*. In 1995 she went to Chittagong for demolition as the *Nac*. These ships also carried 12 passengers.

Frio Brazil -- **Seabridge Shipping Co, Cyprus. (Trevor Jones)**

Kandava -- **USSR-Latvian Shipping Co, USSR; Scott's Shipbuilding Co, Greenock, 1972; 5871gt, 7637dwt, 149m, 3ha, 3x8tn cr, 6x5tn der, 12,000bhp Scott's-Sulzer, 21.25kn. (Tolerton)**

New ownership fails to disguise the distinctive lines of a Geest reefer in these two photographs. The Soviet-flag, Riga-registered *Kandava* (above), desperate for a lick of paint, was originally the *Geestcrest* of 1972, while the *Valparaiso Reefer* (below) was her sister *Geestland* of 1972. Both had accommodation for 12 passengers, six sidedoors port and starboard serving their three holds, and a mix of cranes and derricks.

Valparaiso Reefer -- **Petrikata Shipping Co (International Reefer Services), Malta; Scott's, Greenock, 1972; 5750gt, 7630dwt, 149m, 3ha, 3x8tn cr & 6x5tn der, 12,000bhp Scott's-Sulzer, 21kn. (Trevor Jones)**

Magellan Reefer -- **Aqua Ability SA, Panama; Smith's Dock Co, Middlesbrough, 1981; 10,364gt, 9970dwt, 159m, 4ha, 2x12.5 & 2x8tn cr, 4x5tn der, 13,100bhp Kincaid-B&W, 19.5kn. (Trevor Jones)**

The elegant twin funnel Geest reefers culminated in the *Geestbay* of 1981 and the *Geestport* of 1982, the latter's introduction being interrupted by a call-up as a Falklands war stores ship. Both were passenger "twelves," and they were sold in 1994, the former becoming the *Magellan Reefer*.

St Lucia -- K/S DMK-Femo (Lauritzen Fleet Mgmt), Bahamas; Danyard, Frederikshavn, 1993; 13,077gt, 13,981dwt, 158m, 5ha, 2x36 & 2x20tn cr, 16,515hp Hyundai-B&W, 20.3kn. (Kevin Moore)

Last of the line -- the *Geest St. Lucia* and *Geest Dominica* of 1993 from Danyard and with close affinities with the Lauritzen Family class from the same builder, pictured later in their careers when they were operating for Lauritzen Cool as the Nassau-registered *St Lucia* (above) and *Dominica* (below). Both can carry 439 TEUs, and fuel consumption is 55tn a day.

Dominica -- Geest Ltd (IUM Shipmanagement) Bahamas; Danyard, Frederikshavn, 1993; 13,077gt, 13,981dwt, 158m, 5ha, 2x36tn & 3x20tn cr, 16,507hp Hyundai-B&W, 20.3kn. (Kees Lous)

N class ships like the 3900gt *Nordic* and *Nyantic* of 1984 have been an important part of the Seatrade fleet during the company's growth to prominence in reefer shipping. (Author's collection)

CHAPTER FIFTEEN

SEATRADE GRONINGEN

The rise of Seatrade Groningen BV to a major position in reefer shipping has been one of the features of the last two decades. Established in March 1951 in Groningen as Scheepvaartkantoor Groningen, it was one of many Dutch companies managing small motor coasters, invariably of no more than 500gt, for owner-masters or one ship owners. The company was set up by coaster captain-owners E H Schuur with the *Tempo*, C Lenten with the *Oranje* (and joint owner with Schuur of the *Paramount*), C Tammes with the *Pacific*, R T Tammes with the *Oceaan*, and J Tammes with the *Europa*.

However, the company had the foresight in the 1960s to see that this commerce was dying, and made the move into reefer shipping. Its first reefer was the 1074gt *Arctic* of 1962, followed by the *Tempo* a year later and the *Pacific* (1965) and *Antarctic* (1967) -- all four from the Nieuwe Noord yard in Groningen. The company changed its name to Seatrade Groningen BV in 1973, and in 1976 co-founders E H Schuur, R T Tammes, and C Tammes withdrew from running the company. The new generation of Tom Hammes, Marnix van Overklift, and Henk Schuur, to be joined by Gerry Pepping, took over to steer Seatrade to become one of the big reefer players.

The biggest step came in 1989 when, after the death of its principal Jan Dammers the previous year, Seatrade acquired Dammers & Van der Heide of Rotterdam. Founded in 1945, Dammers & Van der Heide had benefited from the Dutch government's investment programme for shipowners in the late 70s. The takeover doubled the size of Seatrade's fleet and staff. Dammers' six big pallet-friendly 10,500dwt *Honolulu*-class ships and three of the ex-Salen Spring reefers also gave Seatrade a presence in different trades than its own generally much smaller and economical vessels were designed for.

Seatrade's growth continued with the addition of its six 9200gt, 21.5kn Stream class ships from Kitanihon, starting with the *Agulhas Stream* and *Benguela Stream* in 1998, and Seatrade finished the century with about 100 reefers operating for it. While Seatrade's blue funnel with orange houseflag is prominent in the reefer trades, the company has also established itself in recent years as a ship manager for a variety of other vessel types.

Celtic -- Seatrade Groningen BV, Netherlands; Scheepswerf 'Friesland,' Lemmer, 1979; 1198gt, 2468dwt, 81m, 3ha, 1x5tn cr & 4x3tn der, 2500bhp Deutz. (W Plokker)

One of a trio for Seatrade with the *Atlantic* and *Baltic*, the *Celtic* was lengthened by 15m only three years after completion, and renamed *Celtic Ice* in 1989.

Honolulu -- **NV Caribbean Bulk Carriers (Scaldis Reefer Chartering), Netherlands Antilles; Van der Giessen, Krimpen, 1979; 8041gt, 10,598dwt, 155m, 4ha, 4x5tn cr, 16,800bhp Sulzer, 20kn. (Kees Lous)**

Rotterdam owner Dammers & Van der Heide took delivery of the 10,500dwt *Honolulu* (above) in 1979, *Lanai*, *Rio Frio*, and *Christina* in 1980, and *Tineke* (below) and *Peggy Dow* in 1984-85 from Van der Giessen-de Noord, Krimpen, and when Dammers was acquired by Seatrade in 1989 they became the heavyweights of the Groningen fleet. Designed to carry bananas on pallets and all other kinds of reefer cargoes, they also had provision for containers on deck. Four side doors were fitted both port and starboard to serve the four holds, and fuel consumption was 48tn a day. Accommodation was for a crew of 23.

Tineke -- **Tineke Shipping (Scaldis Reefer Chartering), Netherlands Antilles; Van der Giessen, Krimpen, 1984; 11,335gt, 10,510dwt, 155m, 4ha, 4x5tn cr, 16,800bhp Sulzer, 21kn. (Tolerton)**

Reefer Bay -- CSM Reefer Bay Shipping Co (Columbia Shipmanagement (Netherlands)), Antigua & Barbuda; Schpsw Ysselwerf, Capelle, 1982; 1569gt, 3423dwt, 80m, 3ha, 2x3tn cr, 3000bhp Krupp-MaK, 14kn. (Kees Lous)

More typical in size of Seatrade's reefers are the *Reefer Bay* of 1982 (above) and *Joint Frost* of 1979 (below). Built as the *Klipper*, the *Reefer Bay* was one of a series of similar ships from Ysselwerf, Capelle aan den IJssel. Only a 14kn ship, she had fuel consumption of 11tn a day. A similar-sized vessel but a one-off was the 1579gt *Joint Frost* from Brattvag, with three derricks for her three holds. Built for Norwegian owner Sigurd Haavik, she was chartered by Swedish company Joint Travellers, hence the name which she kept when Seatrade acquired her.

Joint Frost -- CV Scheepvaartonderneming 'Joint Frost' (Seatrade Groningen), Netherlands; Brattvag Skipsinnredning, Brattvag, 1979; 1579gt, 2854dwt, 83m, 3ha, 3x5tn der, 3000bhp Bergens-Normo, 14.75kn. (Kees Lous)

Neerlandic -- **Neerlandic NTH Shipping (Thien & Heyenga), Antigua & Barbuda; Schps Gebr van Diepen, Waterhuizen, 1985; 3955gt, 5386dwt, 108m, 4ha, 4x10tn cr, 5500bhp Deutz, 16kn. (Tolerton)**

Waterhuizen builder Scheepswerven Gebroeders van Diepen has had a close association with Seatrade, most notably with the series of seven 3900gt, twin-funnel N class ships built in the mid-1980s, like the *Neerlandic* (above). The yard is inland in Groningen province, and the Ns necessarily had relatively narrow 16m beam to navigate the canals on their first voyage. The *Neerlandic* has three holds and four hatches, served by four 10tn cranes and can carry 93 containers. Manoeuverability is assisted by a controllable pitch propeller and bow thruster, and fuel consumption is 16.5tn a day. She is pictured shortly after swapping the Dutch flag for the flag of Antigua & Barbuda. A later and larger completion for Seatrade from the same yard was the 5918gt *Pacific* of 1996 (below), which had four 7tn cranes and could carry 94 containers.

Pacific -- **CV Scheepvaartonderneming Pacific (Seatrade Groningen), Netherlands; Schps van Diepen, Waterhuizen, 1996; 5918gt, 8500dwt, 133m, 4ha, 4x7tn cr, 9177hp Krupp-MaK, 16.5kn. (Kees Lous)**

Maya -- **Maya Shipping NV (Seatrade Groningen), Netherlands Antilles; Nieuwe Noord, Groningen, 1978; 2989gt, 3547dwt, 101m, 4ha, 4x5tn der, 3000bhp Deutz, 14kn. (Kees Lous)**

The *Maya* of 1978 and lengthened in 1983 was one of a class of eight vessels from Nieuwe Noord Nederlandse Scheepswerven, Groningen -- the yard which built Seatrade's first reefer, the *Arctic*, in 1962. Another manoeuverable little reefer, with controllable pitch propeller and bow thruster and fuel consumption of 11.5tn a day, she was acquired in the Dammers & Van der Heide takeover.

Cape Cavo -- **DS Rendite Fonds Nr.25 ms 'Cape Cavo' GmbH & Co Kuhlschiff KG (Columbia Shipmanagement (Netherlands) BV), Liberia; Shanghai Shipyard, Shanghai, 1991; 6420gt, 6794dwt, 120m, 4ha, 8x10tn der, 9049bhp Shanghai Diesel-Sulzer, 18.4kn. (Tolerton)**

As in other areas of shipbuilding, China is now also contributing to reefer construction. Its first major reefer design is represented by the Liberian-flagged, German KG-owned *Cape Cavo* of 1991, one of several among seven or so reefers built to this design from Shanghai Shipyard which have operated for Seatrade. She is an 6420gt, 18kn ice-strengthened vessel with eight 10tn derricks serving four holds, and able to carry 228 containers (144 on deck and 84 in the holds). Trunked hatches, derricks set high to accommodate the deck containers, and a free-fall liferaft are features of the design.

***Nova Zeelandia* -- Zeerederij 'Holland-Limburg' BV (Seatrade Groningen), Netherlands; Kitanihon Zosen, Hachinohe, 1986; 4440gt, 5508dwt, 115m, 3ha, 5439bhp Akasaka-Mitsubishi, 16kn. (Tolerton)**

As well as its construction at West European yards, Seatrade has augmented its fleet with Japanese-built reefers, like the *Nova Zeelandia* (above), a 1986 completion from Kitanihon Zosen acquired in 1992 after previously trading as the *Mashu Maru* and *Mashu Reefer*. Secondhand Kitanihon-built tonnage has been popular with Seatrade -- the *Nova Liguria* of 1985 (below), built as the *Ligurian Universal* and then the *Ligurian Reefer*, was another completion of similar size from this yard.

***Nova Liguria* - Nova Liguria Shipping Co (Dammers Shipmanagement), Bahamas; Kitanihon Zosen, Hachinohe, 1985; 4361gt, 5459dwt, 109m, 3ha, 6500hp Akasaka-Mitsubishi, 16kn. (Kees Lous)**

Adriatic -- **Adriatic Shipping Co (Seatrade Groningen), Netherlands; Kitanihon Zosen, Hachinohe, 1984; 3505gt, 4173dwt, 99m, 3ha, 6x5tn der, 5400bhp Akasaka-Mitsubishi, 15.5kn. (Kees Lous)**

Two more from Kitanihon, externally differing from the previous pair principally in having a short forecastle: The 3505gt *Adriatic* (above) of 1984 was one of at least six reefers to this design from the Hachinohe yard. She was the *White Reefer* before becoming part of the Seatrade fleet in 1990. The slightly larger *Asiatic* of 1986 (below), previously the *Sanuki Reefer* and acquired in 1991, was yet another Kitanihon completion to see service with Seatrade.

Asiatic -- **Asiatic Shipping Co (Seatrade Groningen), Bahamas; Kitanihon Zosen, Hachinohe, 1986; 3757gt, 4988dwt, 106m, 3ha, 6x5tn der, 4448bhp Akasaka-Mitsubishi, 16kn. (W Plokker)**

Tilapa -- **Empresa Hondurena de Vapores, Honduras; Bremer Vulkan, Vegesack, 1961; 5157/6573gt, 6399dwt, 137m, 4ha, 12x5tn der, 2 X De Lavals steam turbines, 17.5kn. (Keith Byass)**

The *Tilapa* of 1961 was one of six single screw, steam turbine reefers built in 1960-62 by Bremer Vulkan for Fyffes' service but owned by Surrey Shipping Co of Bermuda. In 1973 the *Tilapa* was sold to United Fruit's Honduran subsidiary Empresa Hondurena de Vapores without change of name. Fated like her sisters to a rather abbreviated career because of their steam machinery, she went to the breakers in 1980.

12 May – 10-12 – Archers' Hall visit
  2-4pm Archers' Hall visit
  Dalmeny & Hopetoun
  Jupiter Artland
  Lennoxlove & Newhailes
  Charles Rennie Mackintosh, Glasgow visit Stirling Castle and the Church
  of the Holy Rude
  Undressing Mr Darcy at Winton House *1·15 – 6 pm*

There are changes here c/ou event. Full details ↑ looking
Nedfa Review

15   **AOB** -   Advertising: We have had requests for promoting local galleries etc by displaying/distributing flyers and whilst we are, only too happy to promote small businesses etc, we would agree to leaflets only on seats in the coffee room and on the notice board but not in the hall itself ·

Any extra income from visits, trips etc to go back into BDFAS funds.

Charitable Status – Not agreed upon at present.

Emergency telephone numbers – possible suggestion was printing this on the membership card and the number concerned would, in the event of emergency, have a pre recorded message giving brief details.

16   **Date of next meeting** - Thursday 6th January 2011 at Benrigg, St Boswells at 10am

George Murray (British Army officer)

From Wikipedia, the free encyclopedia

Sir George Murray, GCB, GCH, FRS (6 February 1772 – 28 July 1846) was a Scottish soldier and politician.

Contents

- 1 Background and education
- 2 Military career
- 3 Political career
- 4 Other public appointments
- 5 Personal life
- 6 References
- 7 External links

Background and education

Murray was born in Perth, the second son of Sir William Murray, of Ochtertyre, 5th Baronet (see Murray Baronets), and was educated at the Royal High School, Edinburgh.

Military career

In 1789, Murray obtained a commission into the 71st Foot, reaching the rank of Captain in 1794, and seeing service in Flanders (1794–95), the West Indies, England and Ireland. In 1799 he was made a Lieutenant-Colonel, entering the Quartermaster General's Department and making his considerable reputation as Quartermaster General (1808–11) during the Peninsular War, under the Duke of Wellington, and receiving promotion to Colonel in 1809. After a brief period as Quartermaster General in Ireland, Murray returned to the Peninsular Campaign as Major-General (1813-14), and was invested with the Order of the Bath in 1813. He was briefly in Canada from December 1814 to May 1815 where he was appointed provisional Lieutenant-Governor of Upper Canada and reviewed the defences of Canada. He quickly returned to Europe following Napoleon's escape from Elba, but arrived too late to take part in the Battle of Waterloo.

The Right Honourable
Sir George Murray
GCB, GCH, FRS, PC

Secretary of State for War and the Colonies

In office
30 May 1828 – 22 November 1830

Monarch	George IV William IV
Prime Minister	The Duke of Wellington
Preceded by	William Huskisson
Succeeded by	The Viscount Goderich
Born	6 February 1772 Perth, Perthshire
Died	28 July 1846
Nationality	British
Political party	Tory
Alma mater	None

After cessation of hostilities, Murray was based in France as Chief of Staff to the Army of Occupation and, thereafter, he was appointed Governor of the Royal Military College (1819). He was awarded an honorary degree by the University of Oxford in 1820 and was elected a Fellow of the Royal Society in 1824. In 1825 he married Lady Louisa Erskine, widow of Sir James Erskine of Torrie (1772–1825). Subsequently he was made Lieutenant-General of the Ordnance, but in 1828 he resigned as Commander-in-Chief of the Army in Ireland and became Colonial Secretary. He was later Master-General of the Ordnance between 1834 to 1835 and between 1841 and 1846.

Political career

Murray was a Tory and later Conservative in politics. He was Member of Parliament for Pethshire from 1824–1832 and from 1834 until he retired in 1835. He served as Secretary of State for War and the Colonies from 1828 to 1830. He also contested Westminster in 1837 and Manchester in both 1839 and 1841, without success.

Other public appointments

Murray was also President of the Royal Geographical Society (1833–5) and Governor of Edinburgh Castle.

CHAPTER SIXTEEN

THE GREAT WHITE FLEETS - UNITED FRUIT, CHIQUITA AND FYFFES

Outside of the Cincinnati headquarters of Chiquita Brands, it may be difficult to find anyone proud of the checkered history of its earlier incarnation United Fruit Co, the company synonymous with the "banana republic." However, the history of its Great White Fleet looms large in the story of marine refrigeration and fruitships. That saga looked to have come to an end in May 2007 when Chiquita announced the sale of the last 12 ships of the Great White Fleet.

The Chiquita story started in 1870 when New Englander Lorenzo Dow Baker, master of the fishing schooner *Telegraph*, bought 160 bunches of bananas as extra cargo for one shilling each in Jamaica and sold them 11 days later in Jersey City for two dollars each. That led to a business that soon flourished shipping bananas to Boston where an enterprising partner ashore, Andrew Preston, developed a market for the novel fruit. The pair and other partners created Boston Fruit Co in 1885, still shipping the fruit in fast sailing vessels and reinvesting much of their profits into buying plantations in Jamaica and elsewhere in Central America.

In 1899, with Preston and Captain Baker still prominent, came the creation of United Fruit Co. In less than a year it had absorbed many other banana companies, and a commercial empire with interests throughout the Caribbean and Central and South America, and that could make or break governments, was established.

The ships were white-painted from the start to deflect the tropical sun, and the company's first refrigerated ship was a 26-year-old steamer, the *Venus*, converted in 1903. Experiments with this ship to establish the correct temperatures for carrying bananas in insulated holds led to orders for three new refrigerated ships, the British-flagged coal-fired steamers *San Jose*, *Limon*, and *Esparta*, all delivered in 1904 from Workman Clark, Belfast. Like later United Fruit ships in this trade, they also carried passengers.

Alongside the growth in its own fleet, United Fruit and other American fruit companies from the 1890s through to World War Two chartered dozens of little Norwegian fruitships, naturally ventilated vessels with their decks studded with large ventilator cowls. It was a trade in which many well-known Norwegian shipping names including Klaveness, Staubo, Ditlev-Simonsen, Dahl, and Bergesen as well as future reefer specialists like Kornelius Olsen partially learned the business.

United Fruit also contributed to the development of the flag of convenience with transfers of 13 fruitships from the British flag to Panama in 1928-31. With vessels under the flags of the US, Britain, Honduras, Panama, and the Netherlands, there are some interesting labyrinths for anyone tracing the histories of the ships of United Fruit and its British associate Elders & Fyffes.

By 1939 the Great White Fleet numbered 54 ships under the American, Honduran, and Panamanian flags, plus another 21 ships in the Elders & Fyffes fleet, and United Fruit produced and sold about 65% of the world's bananas.

The American-flag fleet started on a strong footing after the war through the addition of 18 refrigerated steamships built to two standard designs. The first comprised the *Fra Berlanga*, *San Jose*, *Limon*, *Esparta*, *Junior* (all 1945), and *Comayagua* (1946) all built by Gulf Shipbuilding, Chickasaw, Alabama, followed by the *Parismina*, *Heredia*, and *Metapan* in 1947 from Newport News Shipbuilding, Virginia. The second group all came from Bethlehem Steel, Sparrows Point, Maryland -- the *Yaque*, *Cibao*, *Quisqueya*, *Santo Cerro*, and *Sixaola* in 1947 and *Tivives*, *Hibueras*, *Ulua*, and *Morazan* in 1948.

Both designs had four holds and carried 12 passengers. However, the *Fra Berlanga* class were 7074gt, 138m long, twin-screw 18.5kn ships with cruiser sterns and a very extended forecastle, and the *Yaque* class 5075gt, 117m single-screw 16kn ships with counter sterns. By the mid-1950s the fleet served a company that had 40% of the world banana market sourced from more than 1.7 million acres of its own plantations.

However, United Fruit was to encounter stiffer competition from rivals like Dole (formerly Standard Fruit) and Del Monte, and lurched through a number of crises and takeovers. The Chiquita brand, inventively promoted in the 60s, became the company title after Carl Lindner took over and moved the headquarters to Cincinnati. A protracted war with the European Union over banana quotas and some unfortunate business decisions have made times difficult for Chiquita since the early 90s, threatening the future of the famous white diamond funnel in the fruit trades.

In recent years the outstanding addition to the Great White Fleet came with six Nassau-registered 13,049gt, 13,930dwt, 22kn reefers from Danyard based on the Lauritzen Family class -- the *Chiquita Deutschland* and *Chiquita Nederland* (1991), and *Chiquita Belgie*, *Chiquita Schweiz*, *Chiquita Italia*, and *Chiquita Scandinavia* (1992) designed primarily, as their names suggest, for Chiquita's services to Europe.

For more than a century the Great White Fleet has been one of the reefer giants, but in 2007 Chiquita announced the sale of its last 12 vessels -- eight reefers and four container ships -- to Eastwind and NYKLauritzenCool for US$227m. As part of the deal, Chiquita was to charter back 11 of the ships for seven years with an option to extend.

*   *   *

The history of Elders & Fyffes (Fyffes Group from 1969) went hand in hand with that of the Great White Fleet. United Fruit first took a 45% holding in the British company in 1902 and in 1913 it acquired all the company's share capital. And particularly after World War Two there was considerable shuffling of ships from UFC to Fyffes.

Before United Fruit's voyages with its first refrigerated fruitships, the first refrigerated shipment of bananas had been made by a British ship. The *Port Morant* (2830gt/1901) arrived in Bristol in March 1901 with 18,000 stems of bananas from Jamaica. She was one of four small ships built for the new and splendidly named Imperial Direct West India Line, a venture of Elder Dempster Line proprietor Sir Alfred Jones, and created to operate on a 10 years subsidy from the British and Jamaican governments to carry passengers and bananas. Short-lived though this company was, it earned a place in nautical history with the pioneering voyage of the *Port Morant*.

Sir Alfred and trader Thomas Fyffe had separately fostered imports of bananas from the Canary Islands to England in the late 19th century, the former's interest in the potential of this fruit being whetted by his Elder Dempster West African ships topping up with Canary Islands bananas when they coaled at Las Palmas homeward bound. Incorporated in 1901, Elders & Fyffes was another venture of Sir Alfred, but looked to wider possibilities in the Caribbean. As mentioned, United Fruit, sensing a threat, bought a major stake in Fyffes within a year.

After starting with four converted American ships, Elders & Fyffes in 1904 took its first purpose-built banana carrier, the 3872gt *Matina* from Swan Hunter, the first of three sisters, and course was set to make the company (United Fruit's biggest subsidiary) synonymous with both bananas in Britain and passenger services to the Caribbean. When Imperial Direct did not renew its contract, its sister company Elders & Fyffes had this trade to itself.

In any shipping company with a long history, there is some homogeneity to be found in the evolution of its vessels over the years, but probably exceptionally so in the case of Elders & Fyffes' ships with their evocative Central American names. While there were changes in size, design, and propulsion, a visible similarity ran through this fleet from its earliest ships to its completions in the 1960s.

Elders & Fyffes suffered more from World War Two than most companies. It had a fleet of 21 ships in 1939 but lost 14 during the war -- and its London headquarters was destroyed in a bombing raid. The government banned any banana imports during the war (the arrival of the first post-war cargo on the *Tilapa* at Avonmouth in December 1945 was major news), and the Jamaican plantations consequently ran down.

The Fyffes and United Fruit fleets became increasingly interlinked after the war. It was not until the late 1950s that the British company began serious reconstruction, with four 6283gt, 17.5kn ships from Alexander Stephen designed for Fyffes' Cameroon trade, beginning with the *Changuinola* and followed by the *Chirripo* (both 1957), *Chicanoa* (1958), and *Chuscal* (1961). All carried 12 passengers. Fyffes opted for steam turbine propulsion for this quartet, and did the same for its next series, all from Bremer Vulkan, the 6738gt, 17.5kn *Tetela*, *Tenadores*, *Turrialba* (all 1960), *Tilapa*, *Telde* (1961), and *Tucurinca* (1962). Not surprisingly, the C and T class ships had relatively short careers both with Fyffes and subsequent owners. Fyffes' owned fleet was augmented in 1968-70 by the transfer of seven ships from United Fruit, built in the latter's big end-of-war construction programme.

The company, which changed name to Fyffes in 1969, put the steam age behind it and ordered its first ships from Japan with eight 20kn motorships, all from Kawasaki. The first completion was the 6351gt *Matina* of 1969, followed by the *Morant*, *Motagua* (1970), *Musa* (1971), *Manistee*, *Mazatec* (1972), *Magdalena*, and *Manzanares* (1973). The first four had 12 5tn derricks and the next quartet had four 5tn cranes and four 5tn derricks. The last significant class completed for Fyffes' ownership, the Ms were all sold or flagged out in 1982-84.

While Fyffes could be accused of being distinctly conservative with its C and T class construction, it moved quickly, even innovatively, into the container age with the delivery of the Spanish built 4087gt twin-screw motorships *Barranca* and *Bayano* in 1972.

More recent additions were the 4200gt, 16kn *Nickerie* (1985) and *Jarikaba* (1986), followed by the similar 4660gt, 16kn *Coppename* (1990) and *Cottica* (1991), all from Hayashikane, Nagasaki.

Bayano -- Elders & Fyffes, UK; A Stephen, Glasgow, 1917; 6815gt, 118m, 2 x triple expansion steam, 14kn. (Bristol Museums Galleries & Archives)

The *Bayano* of 1917 was Elders & Fyffes' longest serving ship, going to the breakers in 1956 after a 38-year career which included service in the latter part of World War One as an armed merchant cruiser. A 6815gt twin-screw, coal-burning steamer built to carry 104 passengers first class, she typified the graceful combined passenger ship/fruitship running from Avonmouth to the Caribbean for the company, and was estimated to have carried 3000 million bananas to Britain on 280 Atlantic round voyages. She was broken up at Ghent in 1956.

Manistee -- Elders & Fyffes, UK; Workman Clark, Belfast, 1932; 5824gt, 5630dwt, 131m, Workman Clark triple expansion steam. (World Ship Society)

Fyffes acquired the *Manistee* in 1947 as part of the replacement for the 14 ships they lost in the war. She'd been built in 1932 as the *Erin*, one of two sisters for Morant Steamship Co, a British subsidiary of Vaccaro's Standard Fruit of New Orleans. She went to the breakers in 1960.

Reventazon -- **Elders & Fyffes, UK; Deutsche Werft, Hamburg, 1939; 4876gt, 4020dwt, 128m, MAN, 16kn. (World Ship Society)**

Completed in 1939 for Laeisz as the *Panther*, this motorship was state of the art for the banana trade on the eve of the war. Taken over by the Kriegsmarine as the *Salzburg*, she was named, rather unflatteringly, *Empire Mole* when she came under the Ministry of Transport's wing at the end of the war. Elders & Fyffes bought her in 1947 and she gave them 16 years service, her long forecastle and short funnel a contrast to the typical Fyffes steamer. She traded another 10 years before Taiwanese shipbreakers claimed her in 1973.

Matina -- **Elders & Fyffes, UK; A Stephen, Glasgow, 1946; 6801gt, 7583dwt, 135m, 3 x Parsons steam turbines. (World Ship Society)**

Fyffes' post-war construction started with the steamer *Matina* of 1946 from Alexander Stephen, a yard with which the company had a long association, and was designed to carry 170,000 stems of bananas. Fyffes could not be accused of ordering in haste after the war -- she was their only completion until 1956, apart from the passenger vessel *Golfito* of 1949. A Twelve, the *Matina* went to the breakers in 1968.

Fra Berlanga -- **United Mail SS Co (United Fruit), USA; Gulf Shipbuilding, Chickasaw, 1945; 7074gt, 6638dwt, 138m, 4 x De Laval steam turbines, twin screw, 18.5kn. (World Ship Society)**

United Fruit's war design R2-ST-AU1 series of nine 7074gt twin-screw ships from Gulf Shipbuilding, Chickasaw, and Newport News Shipbuilding began with the *Fra Berlanga* of 1945 (above), named after the Dominican friar and 16th century Bishop of Panama who cultivated the first banana plantations. She was scrapped in 1971 in Spain after sinking in dock in Rotterdam. The second was the *San Jose*, also a 1945 completion (below), which became Fyffes' *Ronde* in 1970 and was scrapped in 1976 -- having survived a serious fire during a typhoon off Guam in 1967 and grounding in Honduras in 1972.

San Jose -- **United Mail SS Co (United Fruit), USA; Gulf Shipbuilding, Chickasaw, 1945; 7074gt, 6638 dwt, 138m, 4 x De Laval steam turbines, twin screw, 18.5kn. (World Ship Society)**

Metapan -- **United Fruit SS Corp, USA; Newport News Shipbuilding, Newport News, 1947; 7067gt, 7005dwt, 138m, 4ha, 1x35 & 12x5tn der, 4 x De Laval steam turbines, twin screw, 18.5kn. (World Ship Society)**

Displaying the lines of this class and United Fruit's yellow funnel, red band with white diamond, and black top to perfection is the final completion, the *Metapan* of 1947 (above). She was transferred to the Dutch flag as the *Tinto* in 1970 and broken up five years later. The *Roatan* of Fyffes (below) was built as United Fruit's *Comayagua* in 1946, the last of the six Gulf Shipbuilding completions, and transferred to the British company in 1969. She also went to the breakers in 1975.

Roatan -- **Fyffes Group, UK; Gulf Shipbuilding, Chickasaw, 1946; 6734gt, 6638dwt, 138m, 4ha, 4 x De Laval steam turbines, twin screw, 18.5kn. (World Ship Society)**

Three more of these handsome ships, all in United Fruit's funnel colours. The *Junior* of 1945 (top) became Fyffes' *Rio Cobre* in 1969 and went to Kaohsiung in 1975, while the *Limon* (centre) and *Esparta* (bottom) became the Dutch *Talamanca* and *Toloa* respectively in 1970 and made their last voyages to the same destination in 1977.

Junior -- **United Mail SS Co (United Fruit), USA; Gulf Shipbuilding, Chickasaw, 1945; 7074gt, 6638dwt, 138m, 4ha, 1x35 & 12x5tn der, 4 x De Laval steam turbines, twin screw, 18.5kn. (World Ship Society)**

Limon -- **United Mail SS Co (United Fruit), USA; Gulf Shipbuilding, Chickasaw, 1945; 7074gt, 6638dwt, 138m, 4ha, 1x35 &12x5tn der, 4 x De Laval steam turbines, twin screw, 18.5kn. (World Ship Society)**

Esparta -- **United Mail SS Co (United Fruit), USA; Gulf Shipbuilding, Chickasaw, 1945; 7074gt, 6638dwt, 138m, 4ha, 1x35tn & 12x5tn der, 4 x De Laval steam turbines, twin screw, 18.5kn. (World Ship Society)**

The second group of nine ships were the R1-S-DH1 types, all completed by Bethlehem Steel's Sparrows Point yard within 17 months in 1947 and 1948, with the first being the *Yaque* (below).

These vessels were conspicuous in the post-war decades for their counter sterns, and they were possibly the last significant class of oceangoing ships built with this traditional feature.

Like the *Fra Berlanga* types, the ships of the *Yaque* class were to give United Fruit and its subsidiaries long and largely trouble-free careers. They are ships which for many travelers and mariners represent the picturebook banana boat, beautiful little white-hulled ships bound for the sleepy, palm-fringed anchorages of Central America and the Caribbean.

United Fruit's devotion to steam was of course in contrast to Scandinavian owners of this era with their commitment to the motorship. It is said that the company was convinced the significantly greater vibration transmitted through the hull by diesel engines could damage the bananas.

In the twilight of their careers, some of the R1s and R2s got a new lease of life deployed as Vietnam War supply ships. The *Metapan*, *Sixaola*, and *Cibao*, for example, were all at Qui Nhon in mid-1968 -- probably with more varied cargoes than cynical non-American seafarers' observations about ice cream carriers suggested.

The *Yaque* was transferred to Fyffes and the British flag as the *Patia* in 1970, and went to the breakers a couple of years later.

Yaque -- United Fruit SS Corp, USA; Bethlehem Steel, Sparrows Point, 1947; 5075gt, 5008dwt, 117m, 4ha, 2 x De Laval steam turbines, 16kn. (World Ship Society)

Cibao -- **United Fruit SS Corp, USA; Bethlehem Steel, Sparrows Point, 1947; 5075gt, 5008dwt, 117m, 4ha, 1x20 & 8x5tn der, 2 x De Laval steam turbines, 16kn. (World Ship Society)**

Two more of the *Yaque* class -- the *Cibao*, the second completion (above), and, displaying her counter stern, the *Sixaola*, the fifth (below). The former went in 1970 to United Fruit's Dutch subsidiary Caraibische Scheepvaart as the *Choluteca*, one of a number of United Fruit ships to follow this route, and the *Sixaola* was transferred the same year to Fyffes as the *Patuca*. They were scrapped in 1975 and 1978 respectively.

Sixaola -- **United Fruit SS Corp, USA; Bethlehem Steel, Sparrows Point, 1947; 5075gt, 5008dwt, 117m, 4ha, 2 x De Laval steam turbines, 16kn. (World Ship Society)**

Mardina Importer -- **Faith Shipping Co, Greece; A Stephen & Sons, Glasgow, 1958; 4788/6082gt, 5665dwt, 125m, 4ha, 8x5tn der, 2 x steam turbines, 18kn. (Tolerton)**

The unmistakable lines of a former Elders & Fyffes ship: The Greek steamer *Mardina Importer* (above) was originally Fyffes' *Chicanoa* of 1958 and then *Orica* in 1970 for United Fruit's Honduras subsidiary Empresa Hondurena de Vapores, before being sold to Greek owners in 1972. She went to the breakers soon after this photo was taken in 1974. She was one of four C class single screw, steam turbine "Twelves" built by Alexander Stephen in Glasgow in 1957-61 for Fyffes' then important Cameroon trade, beginning with the *Changuinola* (below). She similarly went to the Honduran flag in 1970 as the *Omoa* and was scrapped in 1975. Fyffes' devotion to steam continued with six T class ships from Bremer Vulkan in 1960-62 for Surrey Steamship Co of Bermuda.

Changuinola -- **Elders & Fyffes, UK; A Stephen, Glasgow, 1957; 4802/6095gt, 5675dwt, 125m, 4ha, 8x5tn der, 2 x steam turbines, 18kn. (World Ship Society)**

Matina -- **Fyffes Group, UK; Kawasaki, Kobe, 1969; 6351gt, 6086dwt, 144m, 4ha, 12x5tn der, 12,600bhp Kawasaki-MAN, 20.5kn. (World Ship Society)**

Fyffes joined the 20th century maritime world in 1969 with the *Matina*, the first motorship ordered by the company and their fourth vessel of this name. She also had the distinction of being their first Japanese-built vessel, and was the first of eight Ms from Kawasaki, Kobe. Innovations included bow thruster and bulbous bow, and she carried six passengers.

Camito -- **Elders & Fyffes, UK; A Stephen & Sons, Glasgow, 1956; 8687gt, 5995dwt, 136m, 4ha, 8x5tn der, 4 x steam turbines, 17.5kn. (World Ship Society)**

The last of Fyffes passenger ships, the twin-screw *Camito* of 1956 carried 103 passengers all in first class accommodation, running from Avonmouth and later Southampton to the Caribbean. She carried up to 140,000 stems of bananas in four holds. Air competition led to a premature demise at a Taiwan shipbreaking yard in 1973.

Chiquita Frances -- **Norvel Ltd (Great White Fleet), Bermuda; Kleven, Ulsteinvik, 1992; 7944gt, 10,963dwt, 140m, 4ha, 4x8tn cr, 16,213bhp MAN, 20kn. (Tolerton)**

Typical of the more recent ships to have operated in the Great White Fleet: The *Chiquita Frances* (above) and *Chiquita Cincinnatian* (below) show off the famous white diamond funnel and Chiquita logo. The former is a sister to the Lauritzen/Erikson "Emperor Penguins" from Kleven, and the latter, built as the *Trans Reefer*, a Japanese standard design from Shikoku. As well as her name being a tribute to owner Chiquita Brands' headquarters city, the vessel's owning company Telegraph Shipping Co was named after founder Lorenzo Dow Baker's famous schooner.

Chiquita Cincinnatian -- **Telegraph Shipping Co (Great White Fleet), Bahamas; Shikoku, Takamatsu, 1984; 6117gt, 6413dwt, 145m, 4ha, 8x5tn der, 7890bhp, 17.5kn. (Tolerton)**

Frio Atlantic 1 -- **Aqua Transports SA (Laskaridis Shipping Co), Panama; 61 Kommunar Shipyard, Nikolayev, 1995; 6964gt, 6685dwt, 133m, 4ha, 8x5tn der, 6959bhp Bryansk-B&W, 16.5kn. (Tolerton)**

The backbone of the Laskaridis fleet had been a class of 6900gt, 16.5kn reefers from the Ukrainian 61 Kommunar shipyard, Nikolayev, where many reefers for the Soviet Union were built. Typical is the *Frio Atlantic 1* (above), which can carry 106 TEUs, with the fenders for ocean fish transshipment prominent on deck. Another ship of this class, the *Frio Poseidon* (below) operates for Riga Transport Fleet, which is 85% Laskaridis-owned after being privatised by the Latvian government in the 1990s, and displays RTF's distinctive gold, blue, and white funnel colours.

Frio Poseidon -- **Global Prestige SA (Riga Transport Fleet), Panama; 61 Kommunar Shipyard, Nikolayev, 1994; 6964gt, 6620dwt, 133m, 4ha, 8x5tn der, 6933bhp Bryansk-B&W, 16.5kn. (Tolerton)**

CHAPTER SEVENTEEN

LASKARIDIS SHIPPING

Low profile Athens-based Laskaridis Shipping Co is another operator to have come to prominence in the last two decades.

Laskaridis has become a leader in fish carrying and ocean transshipment -- traditionally the preserve of Far Eastern and Soviet ships -- while its conventional reefer operations are handled by Alpha Reefer Transport of Hamburg.

A large part of the Laskaridis fleet used to operate under the Cypriot flag, but now it is nearly all Panamanian flagged.

Since the collapse of the Soviet Union, Laskaridis has developed major ventures in that part of the world. It has had a large building programme at the Ukrainian 61 Kommunar shipyard, invested in a Russian fishing fleet, and controls the Latvian Riga Transport Fleet.

The business of brothers Panos and Thanasis Laskaridis is not been confined to shipping -- their group has also invested in airline, hotel, casino, and other interests in Greece, and ship repair yards in Spain.

Frost Olympos -- **Dominion Orientation SA, Panama; Honda Zosen, Saiki, 1983; 4401gt, 4938dwt, 107m, 3ha, 6x5tn der, 6000bhp Akasaka-Mitsubishi, 16.5kn. (Tolerton)**

The white and blue Laskaridis funnel emblem shown on the fish carrier *Frost Olympos* of 1983 – a ship of many names. After previously trading as the *Bungo Reefer*, *Cygnus Reefer*, and *Icicle Reefer*, she became the *Frost Olympos* in 1999, *Idorene Reefer* the same year, then *Recife Bay*, *United Souss*, and *Orca Reefer.*

REEFERS IN COLOUR

Nautical perfection: The classic reefer typified by the *Elsfleth* (1962/4390gt), above, which retained the same name under German and later Greek ownership, and the Ecuadorian *Provincia de El Oro* (1964/8222gt), built as A P Moller's *Magleby Maersk*. (both Tolerton)

J Lauritzen has always had a premier place in reefer shipping. The *Chilean Reefer* (1959/4981gt), above, was part of the Danish owner's 1950s construction programme, which was followed by a very different-looking class which culminated with the *Tunisian Reefer* (1974/5915gt). (both Tolerton)

Representatives of three major classes from the heyday of the Soviet reefer fleet (see also Chapter Four, P59): The *Severnyy Veter* (1969/5093gt), top, one of nearly 40 *Sibir* class fish carriers from 61 Kommunar; the *Larisa Reysner* (1970/5215gt), centre, one of the 12 B443 class reefers from Stocznia Gdanska; and the Latvian *Ivans Kulibins* (ex-Soviet *Ivan Kulibin*) (1976/6400gt), bottom, one of the 14 B437s, also from Stocznia Gdanska. (Tolerton, top and centre, Kees Lous bottom)

Cunard's *Samaria* of 1973 (Tolerton)

BIBLIOGRAPHY AND ACKNOWLEDGEMENTS

I have many people to thank for assistance in the preparation of this book, but especially the Editor of *The Motor Ship* John Barnes, to whom I am profoundly grateful for permission to use some of the publication's splendid ship profiles and plans, Bob Anderson, Mark Andrews, Paul Shackleton, and Tristan Brehaut at publishers WillsonScott, photographers Kevin Moore and Trevor Jones of Durban and Kees Lous of IJmuiden, New Zealand Ship & Marine Society president/secretary Captain Michael Pryce of Wellington for kindly contributing his expertise again, and David Whiteside and Keith Byass of the World Ship Society Photo Library.

Also special thanks to Barbara Jones and Anne Cowne at Lloyd's Register, Andy King (Bristol Museums), Andy Copping, Neil Wheeler, Bruce Carr, Heiko Hartl, Brigitte Morten, Mason Tolerton, Everard Tolerton, Sarah Lee Walker, and to my partner Rosemary Radujko for her patience at times when this project seemed to dominate everything, and the staff of Christchurch Library who always go above and beyond to help.

There are some photographs in the book for which neither the source could be traced nor the photographer contacted, and I offer my apologies and grateful thanks to those individuals.

The following publications were invaluable in compiling this book:

Reference books: *Lloyd's Register of Ships*, *Jane's Merchant Ships*, *Ships In Focus Record* (various vols.), *Significant Ships* (various vols.); Greenway, Ambrose *Comecon Merchant Ships*; Greenway *Soviet Merchant Ships*; Hooke, Norman *Modern Shipping Disasters 1963-87*; Jordan, Roger *The World's Merchant Fleets 1939*; Sawyer, LA, & Mitchell, WH *From America to United States Vol.2*; Stewart, IG *The Ships that Serve New Zealand*; Sigwart, EE *Merchant Ships: World Built* (various vols.).

Books on reefers: Goldberg, Mark *Going Bananas -- 100 Years of American Fruit Ships in the Caribbean*; Hochhaus, Karl-Heinz *Deutsche Kuhlschiffahrt 1902-95*; Kludas, Arnold, & Witthohn, Ralf *Die Deutschen Kuhlschiffe*; Neumann, Peter, & Somer, Jack *Reefership -- The Art and Science of Supplying Fresh Produce to the World*; Parsons, RM *The White Ships -- The Banana Trade at the Port of Bristol*; Pedersen, Hans *La Flotte Frigorifique Francaise*; *Reefer Ships, A Fairplay Guide*.

Company histories: Atkinson, Tony, & O'Donoghue, Kevin *Blue Star*; Bakka Jr, Dag *Hoegh, Shipping through Cycles*; Beaver, Patrick *Yes! We Have Some -- The Story of Fyffes*; Buttkus E, Detlefsen G, Kramer W *Deutsche Reedereien 23, VEB Deutsche Seereederei Rostock*; Cooper J, Kludas A, Pein J *The Hamburg South America Line*; Davies, PN *The Trade Makers*; Detlefsen G *Deutsche Reedereien Band 11*; Harvey, W, & Mackenzie, C *Safmarine*; Haws D *Merchant Fleets: Blue Star*

Line; Holman, Gordon *In the Wake of Endeavour*; Hornby, Ove *'With Constant Care...' AP Moller*; Kolltveit, Bard *Over Linjen, Den Norske Syd-Amerika Linje*; Laird, Dorothy *Paddy Henderson*; Loach, Cyril *A History of the New Zealand Refrigerating Co*; McLellan, R S *Anchor Line*, Morris, Charles *Origins, Orient, & Oriana*; Rabson, Stephen & O'Donoghue, Kevin *P&O, A Fleet History*; Savill, David *Sail to New Zealand*; Thorsoe, Soren *J Lauritzen 1884-1984*; Waters, Sydney *Clipper Ship to Motor Liner*; Waters *Shaw Savill Line*.

Other books: Ambrose AJ *Jane's Merchant Shipping Review* (1 & 3); Birkett, Dea *Serpent in Paradise*; Bock, B & K *Soviet Bloc Merchant Ships*: Kummerman, Henri & Jacquinet, Robert *Ships' Cargo, Cargo Ships*; Villar, Roger *Merchant Ships at War, The Falklands Experience*.

House magazines: *Crossed Flags*, *Denholm News*, *Gangway*, *Lauritzen News*, *Salen-Nytt*.

Periodicals and newspapers: *The Motor Ship*, World Ship Society *Marine News*, *Sea Breezes*, *Ships Monthly*, NZ Ship & Marine Society *Marine News*, *Leading Lights* (Napier branch, NZ Ship & Marine Society), *Bluff Portsider*, Mobil *Compass*, *Time*, *New York Times*.

Websites: Equasis, Miramar Ship Index, Kommandobryggan (Salen).

Asian Lavender **(1998/7355gt), a modern Japanese reefer from Naikai Zosen, owned by Mi-Das Line (Panama) and managed by Doun Kisen. (Tolerton)**

INDEX OF SHIP NAMES

A

Acechilly 85
Acefrosty 85
Aconcagua Valley 23
Adriatic 183
Adriatic Trader 84, 97
Aegean Bay 33
Aegean Progress 33
Aegean Reefer (1964) 22, (1972) 146
Aeolic Reefer 84
African Princess 74
African Reefer (1935) 109, 114, 115, (1985) 111, 113, 118, 123
Afric Star 154, 155, 157
Agulhas Stream 177
Akademikis Vavilovs 48
Akademikis Zavarickis 48
Akademik N Vavilov 48
Akademik Zavaritskiy 48
Alaska 84
Alaskacore 84
Alaunia 85, 93
Albany 22
Albemarle Island 46, 47, 52
Albert Cocozza 225
Albion Star 18
Alcazar Carrier 131
Aleksandra Kollontay 63
Algeciras Carrier 131
Alicante Carrier 131
Almaznyy Bereg 62
Almeda Star 155, 157, 161, 162, 208
Almeria Star 155, 157, 161
Alpina 1 146
Alsatia 85, 93
Altcar 133
Amalia 157
Amalric 145

Amazonas 113
Amazon Reefer 146
Amber Atlantic 80
Amber Star 20
America Freezer 85
American Reefer 111, 113, 118
Ananas 101
Andalucia Star 155, 157, 161, 162, 209
Andania 85, 93
Andria 85, 93
Angelmar 85
Anglian Reefer 111, 113, 141
Anna Salen 129
Anne B 111, 113, 118, 121, 122
Anona 101, 102, 104
Anonacore 100, 101, 102, 206
Antarctic (1967) 177, (1970) 84
Antarcticore 84, 86
Antigua 129
Antilope 130, 133
Anton Gurin 61
Apollonian Champion 112
Apollonian Grace 108, 112
Aquilon 39
Arabian Reefer 110, 112
Arabian Sea 112
Arawak (1952) 129, (1965) 130, 133, (1971) 84
Arctic 177, 181
Arctic C 82, 84, 87
Arctic Goose 112
Arctic Ice (1974) 112, (1989) 141
Arctic Night 112
Arctic Ocean 112, 116
Arctic Reefer 84

Arctic Swan 112
Arctic Universal 77
Argentinean Reefer (1945) 115, (1988) 111, 113, 118, 141
Argolic 85
Argonaut 130, 133
Ariadne 84
Ariane 1 111
Ariel 130, 134
Arkhip Kuindzhi 59
Armonia 85
Arran 157
Asama Maru 73
Asian Lavender 216
Asian Reefer 110, 111, 113, 118, 119
Asiatic 183
Asta 109
Asteri 23
Athenian Reefer 146, 153
Atitlan (1960) 130, 132, (1971) 84
Atlantic Freezer 112
Atlantico 85
Atlantic Ocean 101, 106
Atlantic Star 156, 157, 163
Atlantic Start 157
Atlantic Trader 84
Atlantide 130, 132
Attica Reefer 146
Auckland 79
Auckland Star 156, 157, 164
Australia Freezer 85
Australian Reefer 111, 113
Avelona Star 155, 157, 160, 161, 208
Avila Star (1975) 155, 157, 161, 163, (1990) 166
Avocadocore 99, 101, 102

B
Bagno Catarama 85
Bagno El Triunfo 85, 92
Bagno Esmeraldas 85
Bagno Quevedo 85
Bahamian Reefer 84, 96, 97
Bahiana Reefer 170
Balboa Reefer 84, 94
Baleares 26
Balkan Reefer 110, 113, 118
Ballade 129
Balmar 85
Balmoral Castle 43
Baltic Sky 113
Baltic Snow 113
Baltic Star 156, 157
Baltic Start 157
Baltic Stream 113
Baltic Sun 113
Baltic Universal 77
Baltic Wave 157
Baltic Wind 157
Balzac 18
Bambara 38
Bananacore 99, 101
Banana Planter (1960) 171, (1972) 85
Banana Reefer 85
Banana Trader 44
Bananor 85
Barbara Brovig 19
Barcarolle 129, 224
Barcelona Star 25
Barranca 187
Barrington Island 46, 47
Barrios 74
Basil 18
Bassro Arctic 146
Bassro Nordic 146
Bayano (1917) 11, 188, (1972) 187
Beacon Hill 146, 151
Belgian Reefer (1958) 108, 110, 112, (1974) 120, (1983) 113, 122
Belinda 141
Belnippon 23, 25
Belouga 39
Benadir 28
Benguela Stream 177
Bering 84
Beringcore 84

Betty B 111, 113, 122
Bille Frost 85
Blue Sea 130
Blumenthal (1974) 120, (1983) 57
Bolero 129
Bolero Reefer 146
Bolivar 84
Bolivar Trader 84
Bonita (1968) 112, (1970) 84
Bora Universal 75
Bothnian Reefer 111, 113, 125
Brasilia Reefer 84, 91, 97
Brazilian Reefer (1953) 109, (1975) 120, (1984) 113, 122, 203
Bremerhaven (1975) 120, (1984) 57
Brest 56
Brestskaya Krepost 84
Bretagne 56
Bristol Clipper 85
Brunsbuttel 27
Brunseck 28
Brunshausen 26, 27
Brunsholm 29
Brunsland (1964) 27, 28, (1972) 101
Brunstal 26
Buenos Aires 146
Bungo Reefer 199
Byfjord 17

C
Cacilia B 51
Cadiz Carrier 131
Calarossa 25
Calasetta 25
Camito 196
Canadian Reefer (1936) 114, (1979) 110, 113, 118, 119
Canadian Star 113
Cantaloup 100, 101
Canterbury Star (1960) 145, (1986) 156, 157, 165, 209
Cap Corrientes 146
Cap Domingo 35
Cap Ferrato 84
Cap Frio (1974) 84, 92, (1983) 76
Cap Ortegal 13

Cap Triunfo 77
Cape Cavo 181, 212
Capetan Leonidas 146
Capricorn 101
Carare 11
Cardiff Clipper 85, 93
Carelian Reefer 111, 113, 124
Carib 129
Caribbean Star 167
Carina 101
Carinthia 100, 101
Cariocas Reefer 146
Carlshamn 129
Carmania 100, 101
Carmencita 141
Carroll 18
Castle Peak 157
Castor 101
Cayman (1956) 129, (1971, from Drammen) 84, 87, (1971, from Nylands) 101, 105
Ceiba 101
Celtic 177
Centaurus 100, 101
Chaiten 101
Changuinola 187, 195
Chapayev 44
Charles Island 47
Cherry 100, 101, 105, 107
Chicanoa 187, 195
Chikuma Reefer 79
Chilean Reefer (1959) 110, 112, 115, 202, (1984) 51, 118, (1992) 113, 124
Chillan 101
Chilly 85
Chios Clipper 85
Chios Pride 84
Chios Reefer 101
Chiquita Belgie 186
Chiquita Cincinnatian 197
Chiquita Deutschland 186
Chiquita Frances 197
Chiquita Italia 186
Chiquita Nederland 186
Chiquita Scandinavia 186
Chiquita Schweiz 186
Chiquita Tower 130
Chiricana 80
Chirripo 187
Cholguan 101

Choluteca 194
Christina 178
Chrysantema 100, 101, 107
Chuscal 187
Cibao 184, 194
Circassia 9
Citrus do Brasil 101, 103
City of Durban 13
Ciudad de Guayaquil 84, 85, 87
Clan Ramsay 42, 43
Clan Ranald 43
Clan Robertson 43
Clan Ross 43
Clementina 100, 101, 105
Colombian Reefer 51, 118
Comayagua 186, 191
Comfort 29
Condata 101
Condora 101
Copacabana Reefer 101
Coppename 187
Corfu Reefer 146
Corinto 101
Corrado 1 146
Costa Rican Star 167
Cote d'Ivoirian Star 167
Cottica 187
CR Alicante 56
CR Dieppe 56
Crusader 21
Crux 35
Crystal Pilgrim 52
Crystal Pioneer 52
Crystal Pride 52, 53
Crystal Primadonna 52, 53
Crystal Prince 52, 53
Crystal Privilege 52, 53
Curacao Reefer 85
Cygnus Reefer 199

D
Del Monte Quality 54
Del Monte Trader 166
Delphic Reefer 146, 152
Dimitrios K 21
Ditlev Lauritzen 109, 111, 113, 126, 127
Dole Africa 66
Dole America 66
Dole Asia 66
Dole Chile 13

Dole Colombia 13
Dole Europa 66
Dominica 175
Dora 109
Dover Castle 43
Dragor Maersk 6, 24
Duncan Island 47
Dunedin 10

E
Eboe 9
Ecuadorian Reefer (1962) 110, 112, 116, (1980) 113, 118
Edinburgh Clipper 85, 93
Egyptian Reefer 113
Eisha 85
Elisabeth B 51
Elisabeth Berg 84, 85, 90
Elita 28
Elsfleth 16, 40, 201
Emanuel 82, 84, 95, 205
Emanuel B 82, 84, 95, 205
Emanuel C 84
Empire Mole 189
Encounter Bay 13
English Star 156, 157, 164
Erikson Arctic 141
Erikson Cooler 141
Erikson Crystal 141
Erikson Freezer 140, 141
Erikson Frost 141, 142
Erikson Nordic 141
Erikson Polar 140, 141
Erikson Reefer 141, 143
Erikson Snow 141, 142
Erikson Winter 141
Erin 188
Ernst Moritz Arndt 85
Esparta (1904) 185, (1945) 186, 192
Europa 177
Europa Freezer 85
EW Andes 166
EW Kilimanjaro 121
Extreluz 56
Extresol 56

F
Fair Reefer 112
Fares Reefer 146, 151
Farid F 84

Fastelle 42
Favorita, 39
Fife 157, 162
Flamingo Reefer 146
Fort Carillon 36
Fort Dauphin 36
Fort Desaix 36
Fort La Reine 37
Fort Pontchartrain 37
Fort Richelieu 36
Fort Richepanse 36
Fort Royal 13
Fort Sainte Marie 39
Fortuna Bay 113
Fortune Bay 113
Fra Berlanga 186, 190, 193
Fremantle Star 158, 159
Fribourg 39
Frigoantartico 84
Frigoartico 84, 92
Frigomare, 37
Frigo Oceania 54
Frigorifique 9
Frio Adriatic 101
Frio America 54
Frio Atlantic 1 198
Frio Bahia 33
Frio Bay 33
Frio Brazil 172
Frio Bremen 85, 93
Frio Chile 84, 88
Frio Clipper 85
Frio Hamburg 85
Frio Ipanema 74
Frio Poseidon 198
Frio Progress 33
Frio Venezuela 33
Fritz Reuter 25
Frostfjord 31
Frost Olympos (1980) 54, (1983) 199, 211
Frosty 85
Frozen Lulis 101
Frysna 37

G
Geestbay (1964) 169, 171, (1981) 168, 169, 170, 174
Geestcape 169
Geestcrest 169, 170, 174
Geest Dominica 170, 175
Geesthaven 169

Geestland (1960) 169, 171, (1972) 169, 173
Geestport (1964) 169, 171, (1982) 169, 170, 174
Geeststar 169, 172
Geest St. Lucia 170, 175
Geest-tide 169
Gerhart Hauptmann 85
Gladiola 100, 101
Gladstone Star 158
Glasgow Clipper 85, 93
Golar Borg 84
Golar Freeze 83, 84, 86
Golar Frost 84
Golar Fruit 20
Golar Girl 84, 85, 87
Golar Nel 83, 84, 86
Golar Ragni 84
Golden B 85
Golden Lady 158
Golden Ocean 19
Golden Reefer 146
Gold Medal 131, 135
Golfito 189
Gomba Challenge 225
Grand United 30
Great Eastern 10
Green Austevoll 141
Green Bodo 141
Green Cooler 141
Green Crystal 141
Green Egersund 141
Greenfield 131, 135, 138
Green Freesia 225
Green Freezer 140, 141
Green Karmoy 141
Greenland 84, 87, 204
Green Maloy 141
Green Selje 141
Guava 101, 104
Guavacore 100, 101, 104

H
Hansa Bremen 56
Hansa Lubeck 56
Hansa Stockholm 56
Hansa Visby 56
Haparangi 10
Harlech 157, 162
Hawaii 74
Hawk 25
Hayatsuki Maru 71

Heinrich Heine 85, 92
Helene Jacob 57
Heredia 186
Hibueras 186
Hidlefjord (1960) 17, (1975) 155, 157, 163
Hilco Girl 84
Hilco Scamper 51
Hilco Skater 51
Hilco Skier 51
Hilco Speedster 51
Hilco Sprinter 51
Hispaniola (1956) 129, (1971) 101
Honolulu 177, 178
Hood 130, 136
Hood Island 47
Hood River Valley 23
Hornbay 67
Horncap 67
Horncliff (1973) 146, (1985) 157, (1992) 67
Hornsea (1973) 146, (1986) 157, (1997) 167
Hornsound 157
Hornstream 157
Humboldt Rex 166
Humboldt Rex No.2 166

I
Iberian Reefer (1968) 120, (1985) 56, (1991) 140, 141
Ice Bell 157
Iceland 84
Ice Louise 51
Ice Pilot 31
Ice Ranger 113
Ice River 113
Ice Rose 113
Ice Runner 113
Icicle Reefer 199
Idorene Reefer 199
Ifni 84, 91, 97
Ikoma Maru 73
Imilchil 84, 91
Imouzzer 84
Imperial Star 155
Indian Ocean 112, 116
Indian Reefer 141, 143
Ionic Reefer 84
Iran Mofid 51
Irish Sea 101

Iris Queen 100, 101
Isla Fernandina 84
Isla Genovesa 84
Isla Isabela 85
Isla Pinta 85, 95
Islas Galapagos 45
Itajai Reefer 22
Italian Reefer (1968) 110, 112, 116, (1985) 56, (1992) 141, 143
Ithaka Reefer 84, 204
Itohamu Maru No.1 70
Ivans Kulibins 213
Ivar Lauritzen 111, 113, 126, 203
Ivondro 39

J
Jana 60
Jarikaba 187
Jawaher 85
John Brinckman 23
Joint Frost 179
Jorgen Lauritzen 111, 113, 118, 126
Junior 186, 192
Juvante 80
Juyo Maru 70

K
Kalypso 85
Kandava 170, 173
Karl Liebknecht 62
Karukera 38
Kassos Reefer 101, 104, 206
Kastora 101
Katah 81
King Edmund 85
King Egbert 85
Kinpurnie Castle 43
Kirki 84
Kista Dan 115
Klipper 179
Knud Lauritzen 111, 113, 118, 126
Komsomolskaya Smena 60
Kotovskiy 44
Kungshamn 84
Kurpie 65
Kyma 130
Kyokushin 81
Kyokushin Maru 81

L
Labrador Clipper 84, 91
Lady Madonna 43
Lake Eyre 20
Lanai 178
Lanark 157
Langstone 21
Lapland 84
Lapponian Reefer 111, 113, 124
Larisa Reysner 58, 213
Lemoncore 99, 101
Levante 80
Ligurian Reefer 182
Ligurian Universal 182
Lilia 1 84
Lily 29
Lima 146
Limari 130
Limon (1904) 185, (1945) 186, 192, (1968) 84, 86
Limon Trader 146
Lincoln Universal 77
Liverpool Clipper 85
Liza 44
Loch Lomond 42
Loch Long 42
Loch Maree 42
Loen Stream 55
Lola 33
London Clipper 85
Lucky (1968) 101, (1973) 84
Luhesand 35

M
Macedonian Reefer 146, 152
Magdalena 187
Magellanic 85
Magellan Reefer 170, 174
Magleby Maersk 24, 201
Mahone Bay 67
Mahsuri 146
Mairangi Bay 13
Malaga Carrier 131
Malayan Empress 130
Malayan King 130
Malayan Queen 131, 135
Malibu Reefer 84
Malicia 84
Manapouri 69, 145, 146, 152
Mandama 146, 149
Mandarincore 100, 101

Mangocore 99, 101
Mango Reefer 112
Manila Tiger 121
Manistee (1932) 188, (1972) 187
Manzanares 187
Maracaibo Reefer 146
Maranga 100, 101
Marathon Breeze 146
Marathon Reefer 146
Mardina Importer 195
Mare Boreale 44
Mare I 22
Marko Polo 35
Marsala 10
Marsouin 39
Mashu Maru 182
Mashu Reefer 182
Matangi 11
Mataura (1868) 10, (1968) 69, 145, 146, 152
Matina (1904) 187, (1946) 189, (1969) 196
Maya 181
Mazatec 187
Metapan 186, 191
Metonic 85
Mexican Bay 113
Mexican Reefer (1953) 109, (1994) 111, 113, 123
Milos IV 29
Milos Reefer 101
Minden 29
Minoan Reefer 23
Minoic Reefer 84
Miramar 33
Morant 187
Morazan 186
Morillo 100, 101, 107, 212
Mosdale 18
Motagua 187
Musa 187

N
Nac 172
Nafplio 85
Narval 39
Navelina 101
Navelinacore 100, 101, 103
Naxos Reefer 84
Nectarine 101, 103
Nectarinecore 100, 101, 103

Neerlandic 180
Network Stork 85
Network Swan 85
Newcastle Clipper 85
New Zealand Reefer 76, 110
Nickerie 187
Nienburg 76
Nikolay Kopernik 63
Nikolay Shchors 44
Nippon Reefer (1970) 39, 110, 112, 116, (1982) 76, 118
Nissos Naxos 84
Nissos Paros 84
Nissos Skiathos 84
Nissos Skopelos 84
Noor 130, 131, 136
Nordenham 76
Nordic 176
Nordic Bay 85
Nordic Cape 84
Nordic Ice 85
Nordic Star 84
Nordice 141
Nordland 82, 84, 87
Norfolk 9
Norman Star (1939) 18, (1979) 166
Northam 9
North Star 171
Nova Liguria 182
Nova Zeelandia 182
Nyantic 176

O
Oceaan 177
Ocean Breeze 65
Ocean Bride 76
Ocean Freezer 112
Ocean Ice 74
Ocean Pride 76
Oceania Freezer 85
Oceanic Trader 76
Oceano Artico 72
Okanagan Valley 23
Olancho 101
Olympian Reefer 146
Omoa (1957) 195, (1964) 101
Ondine 40
Orange 100, 101
Orange Star 157, 161
Oranje 177

Orca Reefer 199
Orchard Gold 30
Orchidea 100, 101
Orenoco Reefer 85
Orica (1958) 195, (1965) 101, 102
Orient 10
Orpheus 40
Otomar Oshkaln 64
Otrant Frigo 84, 97
Ouro do Brasil (1970) 101, 103, (1993) 50

P
Pacific (1965) 177, (1996) 180
Pacific Express (1945) 18, (1964) 25
Pacific Fruit 29
Pacific Governess 50
Pacifico 85
Pacific Ocean 24
Pacific Reefer (1935) 109, 114, (1974) 72
Pacific Star 156, 157
Pacific Start 157
Pacific Trader 84
Padova Star 25
Panther (1939) 189, (1979) 74
Paquisha 85, 94
Paraguay 9, 10
Paramount 177
Parana 113
Parismina 186
Parkhomenko 44, 58
Parthenon 25
Pasadena 101
Patia 193
Patuca 194
Pecan 100, 101, 104
Pegasus 101
Peggy Dow 178
Pelagos 101
Pentelikon 30
Pentland Phoenix 78
Perseus 101
Persian Reefer 110, 112, 117
Persimmon 30, 31
Persimmoncore 100, 101
Perth 157
Peruvian Reefer (1954) 109, (1970) 110, 112, 117, 118,

(1992) 113, 125, 204
Pioner 30
Piraus 25
Pisang 31
Plencia 120
Plod 30
Pocahontas 31, 226
Pocantico 31, 67
Polar Argentina 32
Polar Brasil 32
Polar Chile 66
Polar Colombia 32, 33
Polar Costa Rica 34, 153
Polar Ecuador 32
Polar Honduras 34, 153
Polar Paraguay 32
Polar Uruguay 32, 33
Polluks 64
P&O Nedlloyd Remuera 12, 13
Port Caroline 10
Port Chalmers 10
Port Morant 8, 10, 186
Port St Lawrence 11
Portugalete 120
Portunus 30
Potomac 31
Pride III 85
Professor Popov 63
Proliv Longa 61
Protos 10
Provincia de El Oro 24, 201
Provincia del Guayas 84, 87, 205
Provincia de Los Rios 112
Puerto Cabello 84
Puma 74
Punente 80
Pungo 30

Q
Quadrivium 26
Quartole 26
Queensland Star 158
Quisqueya 186

R
Racisce 67
Ragni Berg (1972) 84, (1978) 84, 96
Rainbow Star 37
Ranada 18
Rauma Reefer 113

Recife Bay 199
Reefer Badger 121
Reefer Bay 179
Reefer Ciku 84
Reefer Duku 84
Reefer Jambu 111, 113
Reefer Manggis 84, 90
Reefer Nangka 84
Reefer Penguin 78, 110, 111
Reefer Princess 146
Reefer Queen 81
Reefer Rio 22
Reefer Sun 157
Reefer Tiger 110, 121
Reifu 15
Remuera Bay 13
Reno 85
Republica del Ecuador 101, 106, 206
Resolution Bay 13
Rio Amazonas 45
Rio Babahoyo 84, 85, 94, 95
Rio Chone 84, 94
Rio Cobre 192
Rio Daule 84
Rio Esmeraldas 84, 94
Rio Frio 178
Rio Guayas 101
Rio Negro Valley 23
Rio Santa Rosa 85
Rizhskiy Bereg 62
Roatan 191
Robur 129
Rockhampton Star 158, 159
Roman Hurricane 85
Roman Reefer 110, 112, 116, 118
Ronde 190
Ronirel 29
Rosemary 101, 104
Royal Lily 13
Royal Sea 225
R P Cayman 101

S
Sabracore 100, 101
Salinas 85
Saltlake 81
Salzburg 189
Samaria 100, 101, 107, 214
Samoan Reefer 110, 112, 117
Samos Sea 3, 20

Samos Sun 20
San Benito 130, 133
San Blas (1955) 129, (1967) 131, 133
San Bruno 130, 133
Sandhamn 129
San Joaquin Valley 23
San Jose (1904) 185, (1945) 186, 190
San Nicolas 39
Santiago Star 131, 135
Santo Cerro 186
Santos Star 131, 135
Sanuki Reefer 183
Saracen 21
Satsuma 101
Satsumacore 100, 101
Savona Star 131, 135
Savonian Reefer 111, 113, 125
Saxonia 100, 101
Saxon Star (1979) 166, (1983) 57
Scandinavian Reefer 111, 113, 124
Scirocco Universal 75
Scottish Star 154, 156, 157, 163, 164
Scythia 100, 101
Sea Sovereign 129
Segovia Carrier 131
Sergey Lazo 44
Servia 102, 101
Severnyy Veter 213
Sevillan Reefer 120
Sibir 60, 213
Sierra Lara 55
Sierra Laurel 55
Sierra Leyre 55
Sierra Loba 55
Sierra Nevada 84
Sijilmassa 84
Silver Reefer 146
Silver Tower 130, 207
Sixaola 186, 194
Skiathos Reefer 84, 86
Skulptor Tomskiy 48
S.Lucia 84
Smara 84
Snow Ball 131, 135
Snow Cape 131, 135
Snow Crystal 131

Snow Delta 130
Snow Drift 131, 134, 135, 138
Snow Flake 130, 135
Snow Flower 130, 134
Snow Hill 130, 131, 136
Snow Land 130, 207
Snow Storm 130, 136
Sol do Brasil 101
Sonoda Reefer 72
South Cathay 131, 135
Southern Universal 118
South Fountain 130
South Joy 131, 135
South View 130
Soyokaze 71
Soyokaze Maru 71
Spring Ballad 131
Spring Bear 131
Spring Bee 131
Spring Bird 131
Spring Blossom 131
Spring Bob 131
Spring Bok 131
Spring Breeze 131
Spring Bride 131
Spring Deli 131
Spring Delight 131, 138
Spring Desire 131
Spring Dragon 131
Spring Dream 131
Spring Panda 131
Spring Tiger 131
Star Light 101
Starsea 84
Stina 157
St Lucia 175
Strathleven 10
Suco do Brasil 101
Sultana 100, 101
Sultanacore 100, 101, 103
Sun Swan 157
Swan Lake 157

T
Table Bay 13
Tajin 120
Talamanca 192
Tangelo 100, 101, 106, 206
Tangerinecore 100, 101
Tasmanic 130
Tasman Rex 166

Tasman Star 156, 157
Tasman Start 157
Tasman Universal 77
Tatarstan 60
Taupo 144, 145, 146, 148, 149, 150, 152
Taveuni 115
Tbreed III 84, 97
Tbreed VII 84, 95
Teesside Clipper 85, 93
Tekoa 145, 146, 148, 149
Telde 187
Telegraph 185, 197
Tempo 177
Tenadores 187
Tetela 187
Theodor Korner 85
Thorbjorg 78
Thorgull 78
Thuro Maersk 24
Tilapa 184, 187
Timur Girl 84
Tineke 178
Tinto 191
Tivives 186
Tokyo Reefer 73
Toloa 192
Tongariro (1883) 10, (1967) 145, 146, 148
Torrens 84
Townsville Star 158, 167
Trajan 66
Trans Reefer 197
Trojan Star (1973) 85, (1984) 57, 157
Tropical Breeze 85
Tropical Estoril 84
Tropical Land 101
Tropical Sintra 84, 92
Tropicana Reefer 84
Tucurinca 187
Tudor Star 57, 157
Tundra Queen 54
Tundra Trader 166
Tunisian Reefer 110, 112, 117, 118, 202
Turakina 145, 147
Turbo 74
Turrialba 187
Tuscan Star (1972) 84, 91, (1973) 146

U
UB Pearl 85
UB Polaris 84, 97
UB Prince 84
UB Prudent 85
Ulla 109
Ulua 186
Union Reefer 112
United Souss 199
Urucitrus 84
Uruguayan Reefer 111, 113, 123

V
Valencia Carrier 131
Valiant Reefer 101
Valparaiso Reefer 173
Velarde 41
Velazquez 41
Venture Reefer 101
Venus 185
Verdaguer 41
Vergina Reefer 84
Vista 1 85
Voce 24

W
Walili 75

Walter Jacob 57
Wan Chun 18
Wellington Star 113, 125
Westmorland 145, 146, 148, 150, 151
White Reefer 183
Wild Auk 145, 146, 153, 155
Wild Avocet 146, 152, 153, 155
Wild Cormorant 34, 146, 153
Wild Curlew 34, 146, 153
Wild Flamingo 83, 84, 88, 146
Wild Fulmar 83, 84, 88, 146
Wild Gannet 83, 84, 88, 89, 90, 146
Wild Grebe 83, 84, 88, 89, 146
Wild Mallard 145, 146, 152
Wild Marlin 145, 146, 152
Winchester Castle 43
Winchester Universal 43
Win Master 71
Winter Moon 131, 137
Winter Sea 131
Winter Star 131
Winter Sun 131, 207
Wintertide 141

Winter Water 131
Winter Wave 131, 137
Wisida Arctic 141
Wisida Frost 141
Wisida Nordic 141
Wisida Snow 141
Wisida Winter 141

Y
Yakima Valley 23
Yanis Lentsmanis 64
Yaque 186, 193, 194
Yrsa 109, 114

Z
Zaida 147
Zain Al-Qaws 85, 90
Zante Reefer 101
Zenit Moon 131
Zenit Sea 131
Zenit Star 131
Zenit Sun 131
Zenit Water 131
Zenit Wave 131
Zira 147
Zyrardow 65

A reefer curiosity -- the 6758gt *Ithaki Kathara*, built in 1962 at La Ciotat as the *Barcarolle*, was one of a steam turbine-powered trio for Salen almost unique in the Scandinavian reefer fleet. Sold after only 10 years to Greek owners, she went to Taiwanese shipbreakers seven years later.

Royal Sea -- Urbino Corp (Spidem Maritime), Greece; Maua, Rio de Janeiro, 1968; 4231gt, 4322dwt, 126m, 4ha, 4x5tn cr, 8400bhp Pesada-MAN, 18.5kn. (Tolerton)

Two reefers with unusual histories -- the *Royal Sea* (above) was built in Brazil, and the *Green Freesia* (below) in India. From the Maua shipyard, the *Royal Sea* was completed for domestic owner Alianca as the *Alberto Cocozza* in 1968 and sold in 1977 to become the *Inga Polaris* before a further sale three years later to Greek owners as the *Royal Sea*. Pictured in German owner Scipio's colours, she was lost in collision in Vietnamese waters in 1993 as the *Pan Harvest*. The *Green Freesia* was built by Mazagon Dock as the *Gomba Challenge*, a general cargo ship, and with four sisters converted and lengthened at Amsterdam in 1984. She became part of the Green Reefers' fleet in 1994 and was sold to become the *Frio Baltasar* in 2002. The growth of Norwegian operator Green Reefers' fleet of small and medium-sized secondhand conventional reefers has been a feature of reefer shipping in the past decade.

Green Freesia -- Green Freesia Corp, Bahamas; Mazagon Dock, Mumbai, 1978; 3677gt, 4299dwt, 107m, 3ha, 2x12.5 & 1x10tn cr, 3180hp Alpha, 14kn. (Kees Lous)

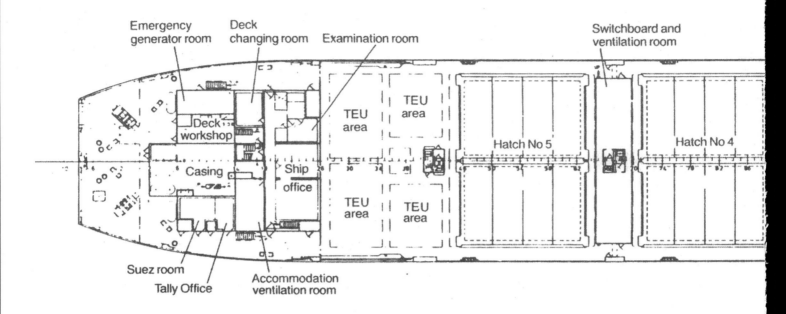

Emergency generator room   Deck changing room   Examination room   Switchboard and ventilation room

Deck workshop

TEU area

TEU area

Casing

Ship office

Hatch No 5

Hatch No 4

TEU area

TEU area

TEU area

TEU area

Suez room

Tally Office

Accommodation ventilation room

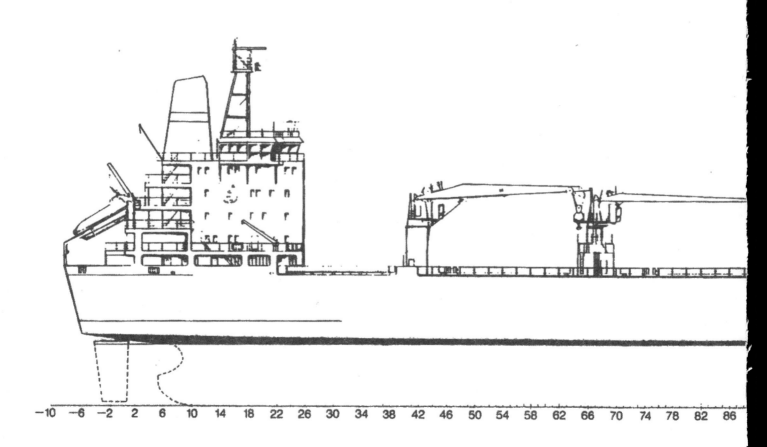

-10   -6   -2   2   6   10   14   18   22   26   30   34   38   42   46   50   54   58   62   66   70   74   78   82   86